THE
JUILLIARD REPORT
on Teaching the Literature
and Materials of Music

THE
JUILLIARD
REPORT

on Teaching the Literature and Materials of Music

GREENWOOD PRESS, PUBLISHERS
WESTPORT, CONNECTICUT

CONTENTS

———•◆•———

INTRODUCTION

BY WILLIAM SCHUMAN,
President, Juilliard School of Music

———————◄•►———————

THESE pages which I am privileged to write are personal,
in contrast to the objective reports of the Juilliard faculty which constitute the subject matter of this volume.
In order to describe how the Literature and Materials of
Music program came into being, I shall have to be slightly
autobiographical. My principal reason for writing this Introduction is, however, to speak of the remarkable teachers who have made possible the development of my own
theoretical concept into a living actuality and to emphasize
that without their unique individual and collective qualities, the program could not possibly have been launched.

When I began teaching in a liberal-arts college in my
twenties, the situation necessitated the development of
teaching techniques and procedures to fit the particular
educational experiment I was engaged to undertake. This
experiment was in the nature of an exploratory freshman
course, dealing with the arts. While my own field of music
was used as the core of the course, the visual arts and
theatre (including dance) were professionally represented
by colleagues from these fields who collaborated in the
experiment, presenting their materials in ways which
paralleled my approach in the music studies.

The course was designed for students who had little or no knowledge of the arts but were sufficiently curious to find out whether they could become interested. It is difficult to imagine any group of students more diametrically opposed to students of Juilliard, or for that matter, any other professional school. And yet it was with this group of students that I began the experiments that led ultimately to the curriculum with which this book deals.

Unlike the liberal-arts student with his comparative lack of motivation and frequent superficiality, the young professional is already vocationally motivated. Despite this wide gulf, the basic stuff that makes up the study of an art for both kinds of student differs only in degree, not in kind. Standards and techniques reflect the quality of a teacher. Meeting the varying needs of students (either professional or lay) entails flexibility on the teacher's part, and the flexible teacher can vary the scope and intensity of the application of standards and techniques, without compromising either the ideal or the need to recognize differences in students. For the student in the liberal-arts college, the emphasis may well be largely upon subjective standards; that is, the use that can be made of the materials of art to help in the intellectual as well as over-all development of the individual student. In the professional school, however, the emphasis is usually exclusively on objective standards of achievement.

It is my basic belief that even for the training of a student with vocational aspirations in the field of music, teaching must be related to an individually adjusted combination of objective and subjective standards. Admittedly, a student with professional goals must achieve results that measure up objectively if he is to function successfully in the particular branch of music he has chosen. Even so, it must be recognized that choice of varying professional goals in music implies expected differences in objective achievement. A concept of music education which combines the seemingly disparate but actually complementary use of subjective and objective standards gives a sound basis for helping each individual student towards the highest degree of achievement of which he is capable.

During the years I taught at Sarah Lawrence College I found that the conventionally designed music curriculum, especially its theory courses, failed to meet the needs of the situation there. I learned very quickly that for education to be meaningful the student had to undergo an emotionally valid experience. While I am not qualified to know whether such a statement applies to other fields, in music an absence of a "felt" reaction means that the composition, even if its techniques were understood, did not "register" with the student. This point of view may be open to challenge, but my experience with many students over the years and with listeners in general, as well as the opinion of a number of exceptionally fine teachers, convinces me that this concept is valid. This should not be misconstrued to mean that the study of music can be a non-intellectual pursuit—an emotional bath—but rather that "feeling" includes the "sensed" application of all intellectual data to the living organism of the art.

With increasing experience as a teacher, I found over and over again that success with my students was directly related to the choice of materials that proved meaningful to them. The methods and techniques of teaching had constantly to be varied not only for the private student in conference, but for classes as well. It became apparent that there could be no set formula for teaching, no rigid curriculum, no unalterable plan of instruction—in short, no supersyllabus which could supply a satisfactory answer to the myriad problems of education. Education, like self-discipline, is never wholly achieved, but is a perpetual, self-generating process. There is no such intellectual finality as having "had" a subject or having "finished." Yet it is equally true that education, notwithstanding its essential need of appropriate fluidity, must be conceived within a framework of absolute and unchanging values. I shall refer to these values at the end of this chapter.

Specifically, my experience led me to challenge the way in which the theory of music was conventionally taught and to adopt more flexible techniques. When subsequently I met with the Board of Directors of Juilliard School of Music, I formulated this experience as I believed it could apply to a professional music school. As with many other music schools and college music departments with whose curricula I was familiar, I felt that at Juilliard the level of the curriculum for theoretical studies was not commensurate with the high level of major instruction in the performing fields. I should like to say here that the Board of Directors not only invited me to develop a program along the lines of my convictions but has given me every support and encouragement in the educational projects we have undertaken. I mention this because school and college boards are so often publicized as ultraconservative and not as groups of forward-looking men such as those with whom it has been my great good fortune to work.*

Beginning with my third year at Juilliard, we replaced the existing theory curriculum with the newly designed curriculum for teaching the Literature and Materials of Music. An article in the April 1948 issue of *The Musical Quarterly* described the beginning of this program, summarized the need for a new approach to theory, and outlined some of the early planning in launching it. My principal collaborator in designing the curriculum was Norman Lloyd, who had been my colleague for a number of years at Sarah Lawrence College and who came with me to Juilliard. The basic concept and the basic design of the curriculum have not changed, although there have been an infinite number of variations in the original plan and there will undoubtedly continue to be such variations in the future. Our biggest problem was to find teachers of sufficient breadth to carry out the concept. Since the plan emphasized the *oneness* of music, it was essential to discover teachers with an expert grasp of the component parts of the art of music without loss of the view of the whole. Furthermore, it was necessary to assemble a faculty for this Department which—while not

* The Directors at the time of my appointment were: Franklin B. Benkard, Henry S. Drinker, John Erskine, Edward Johnson, Parker McCollester, John M. Perry, James P. Warburg, and Allen Wardwell. Upon the deaths of Messrs. Perry and Erskine, John W. Drye, Jr. and Edward R. Wardwell accepted appointments to the Board.

necessarily sharing esthetic convictions or agreeing on precise teaching procedures—would, nevertheless, embrace the basic ideas of the new curriculum.

We were delighted to find, as we began our search, that the teachers of composition at Juilliard were ready to join wholeheartedly in the new plan. These men were composers as well as theorists and it was soon apparent that composers were the best group from which to choose the kind of teachers we desired. This is not strange, for the composer's basic training is concerned with knowledge of and interest in the *language* of music. While this interest and knowledge are also an important part of the art of performance, performers are primarily concerned with the technical skills of performance, whereas the primary interest of composers lies precisely in the technical skills of language. However, since the goal of theoretical instruction, outside the field of composition itself, is to produce more enlightened performers, it was essential that the composer-teachers selected should have a sympathetic understanding of the problems of musical performance. Accordingly, a number of composers were appointed to the faculty, all of them, incidentally, highly skilled performers. The few non-composers appointed were scholars who had been closely identified with creative music. The completion of these appointments meant that the Literature and Materials of Music (Theory) Department then had a faculty of distinction comparable to the artist-teachers in the performing fields at Juilliard.*

Several months before the first classes were scheduled, the entire Literature and Materials of Music Faculty was

* The entire Juilliard Faculty is listed in Appendix 5.

brought together for a series of meetings. It was made clear to the teachers collectively, as it already had been individually, that the Administration would be guided by the Faculty in the realization of its plan for the new Literature and Materials of Music Department. The group was divided into a number of committees which dealt with specific aspects of the Literature and Materials of Music program, reporting back to the entire group and the Administration. This process of meeting, of discussion, of criticism, of group action in collaboration with the Administration, has characterized the spirit in which this educational program developed and functioned. From the beginning, Richard Franko Goldman has served as Secretary for the Department, keeping a running account of the development of the curriculum and keeping the periodic records submitted by the various faculty members. During the first years all the teachers of the Department met with the Administration in regular meetings. More recently, the Department has been guided by a Planning Committee consisting of Assistant Dean Frederick Prausnitz and Messrs. Goldman, Hart, Lloyd and Persichetti, with other teachers, Dean Mark Schubart and myself attending from time to time. With the basic work of planning the curriculum completed and with the valuable experience of a number of years of actual operation, we are returning to the practice of more frequent meetings of the entire Literature and Materials of Music Faculty. Mr. Goldman has been appointed Chairman of the Department to work as direct liaison with the Administration. It is planned to continue a consistent pattern of critical evaluation.

The creative part played by the Faculty in the development of our concept of music education is well illustrated by this book. While this volume carries no authorship credit, the actual writing and collating of material is the work of Mr. Goldman. A copy of the first draft of the book was given to each member of the Department with the request to study it and prepare a list of suggested changes. The manuscript was discussed page by page by the entire Literature and Materials of Music Faculty and in so far as it is humanly possible, the book truly represents the work of a group—the Faculty and Administration. (Copies were also placed in the Library for members of the Faculty at large to peruse and comment upon.)

The Literature and Materials of Music Department as we have organized its actual day-to-day operation represents, in the diverse teaching methods and organization of subject matter, the application of a point of view and not the imposition of a uniform system. This lack of uniformity has caused some confusion in minds accustomed to the usual rigidity of courses in music theory, and students who have been trained through such courses expect and even demand the authority of a "system" that supplies undisputable answers. Traditionally, a "system" gives comfort through textbooks and lectures neatly divided into weekly subdivisions for the length of the school year, and the apparent assurance that a certain amount of factual information has been absorbed. It is not surprising, therefore, that we have received requests for teachers who can "give" the "Juilliard Literature and Materials of Music system." We explain in each instance that we are

not dealing in packaged education, that we have no com-
modity for sale, that far from holding or having applied
for a patent on our "invention," we have no proprietary
interest in guarding our "product," and that we are delighted to make any or all of our findings available to
interested persons. Inquiries from other schools are especially welcome, for it is our conviction that the point of
view represented by our Literature and Materials of Music
curriculum can be applied to the teaching of music any-
where.

Training the amateur in the music departments of institutions of higher education is not only a challenging
field, but one of tremendous importance to the development of the art of music in this country. As I have indicated earlier, there is, to my mind, no excuse for the
training of the amateur to be on a less serious plane than
that of the professional, however varied may be the scope
and intensity of the education. Fortunately, college music
departments more and more are being staffed by skilled
and enlightened musicians who know how to teach and
the day of the vacuous travelogue type of music-apprecia-
tion course with its over-romanticizing is disappearing,
even if the pace is too slow to satisfy some of us. Yet
despite the important advances achieved in the last several
decades, offerings in music in many liberal-arts colleges
still gravitate towards one or the other of two unfortunate
extremes: the general course of music appreciation or
"Introduction to Music," and the theory courses. In the
instance of the general course, many enlightened young
college music enthusiasts are discouraged by being given
a music-history course in which they are subjected to

constant quizzing on dates and factual data, or an "analysis" course in which they are obliged to memorize what are purported to be rigid forms as the key to listening to music. In the standard theory course, the young student who loves music is likely to be discouraged by the routine of writing abstract harmony exercises whose musical application he fails to glean.

In contrast, how dynamic would be the college music course which set aside preconceived notions of the rigid organization of music into history, analysis, and theory, to present music as a whole in a manner calculated to exploit the student's love of it and his desire for training! To be sure, there are liberal-arts colleges whose music departments aim to do precisely this, but even some of these are hampered by continuing adherence to the heritage of conservatory curricula carried over from Europe. Because of these considerations, it is especially in the liberal-arts college that I believe a point of view based on the approach of the Juilliard Literature and Materials of Music curriculum can be effective.

To improve education takes more than dissatisfaction with the status quo. The evolution of a curriculum requires willingness to deal not only with the unknown, but with the inconvenient. It means, in our oversystematized world of education, a profound disrespect for the clerical end of educational accounting (number of hours and points per course, transfer credits, etc., etc.) and a determination to make such inescapable chores bend to an educational ideal and not to permit them to block it. At a meeting not long ago, attended by teachers from music departments of a number of liberal-arts colleges, there was open discussion of the methods employed in various professional schools, including Juilliard. While some teachers were quick to sense the comparative values of the various programs discussed, it was discouraging to find that many permitted clerical difficulties to dominate their thinking.

A professor of theory from the school of music in one of our large universities who recently made a thorough study of the Juilliard Literature and Materials of Music curriculum was kind enough to let me see a copy of the report he submitted to his administration. In his report, the point was made that the curriculum as organized at Juilliard was fine for Juilliard but that it could not be applied *in toto* at his particular school. Nevertheless, believing as he did in the fundamental premise of the Juilliard program and in the kind of teachers who conducted it, he was searching for ways to enable his own school to move in a similar direction. This represents to my mind the most practical approach to the adaptation of the essence of an educational idea to a local situation. It should be a natural and continuing part of education in music that ideas be exchanged and applied with appropriate modifications in other institutions. There is an astonishing amount of conformity in the field of higher musical education by institutions with different educational aims.

It has been of great interest to learn of the reactions of colleagues in music education to this experiment. These reactions at first tended to extremes, ranging all the way from unthinking approval to blind rejection. In retrospect it is difficult to understand what formed the basis for these often passionate reactions since they came immediately with our preliminary announcement of the intention of changing the theory curriculum. Those who reproved and those who approved, both, did so without any possible means of knowing what we were going to do except that we planned to change the curriculum. Often, too, the reactions which we were privileged to hear concentrated on extrinsic speculations—for example, on whether or not the program was, in fact, NEW. Whether what we are doing is old or new has little bearing on its validity and at no time has the issue of "novelty" even been discussed, let alone considered. I suppose that what we are doing is at once both old and new. It is old in the sense that it embodies the truth that enlightened teachers have always taught in their own spheres of time, place, and subject, on the basis of an educational concept akin to that of our Literature and Materials of Music Department. What we are doing is new in the sense that, to our knowledge, there has been no previous attempt to launch a curriculum based on this point of view in a music school. Whether the program is old or new, serious interest in it is very much in evidence.

We are greatly encouraged by the increasing number of colleagues who visit Juilliard in order to make a serious study of what we are attempting to do. We welcome such visitors, always suggesting that they stay at the School a sufficient length of time to observe a number of teachers, as well as to talk at their pleasure with students. Occasionally, outsiders who have studied the Department are kind enough to share their reactions with me. All the comments I have received from them, both written and oral, stress the remarkably gifted teachers of the Literature and Materials of Music Department. Nothing is more gratifying than this recognition of the outstanding quality of our teachers. While it is not possible to describe their teaching in words (something of their range in musical materials and the breadth of their interests can be gleaned from the body of this report), it is not too much to suggest that they have given a new dimension to the study of music outside the performing areas. No individual teacher can or does pretend to all-inclusive knowledge, but we feel that our curriculum is so designed that we are able to free for use the total knowledge of each individual teacher as well as the sum of the knowledge and experience of the group as an entity. Teaching the Literature and Materials of Music demands active participation or involvement with music as a continuing study, plus the desire and ability to teach. Fortunately, Juilliard has no monopoly on fine teachers, and it is obvious that there are many teachers in other schools who would be most effective in a curriculum similar to ours. Furthermore, I know from personal experience that fine teachers can bring a creative approach to the most routine curriculum, and conversely, that no curriculum, however fine its planning, is better than the teachers concerned. We believe that the Literature and Materials program in the hands of gifted teachers can imbue the student with a living sense of music's language and can transform what is often the dreary study of music theory into the excitement of discovery.

While the Literature and Materials of Music approach to theory could be adapted for use in colleges and even in secondary and elementary schools, it must be borne in mind that in organizing and launching this program of studies at Juilliard we have had an ideal situation. As is made amply clear in the following pages, one of the unique features of the Literature and Materials of Music approach to the teaching of "theory" is the consistent emphasis on performance. The situation at Juilliard is ideal because we have had the advantage of co-operation with the artist-teachers of the School, not only as performers but, of course, as teachers. As performers, they have frequently participated and their co-operation in teaching has made possible literally hundreds of performances on the part of gifted students for the Literature and Materials of Music classes. In addition, the School bursts at the seams with all manner of musical activity ranging from full-scale opera, symphony, and chorus to variegated chamber-music ensembles and solo performances. It is not this wealth of performing talent alone that creates value; it is the use to which it is put in the realization of our attitude towards repertory. This attitude insists on an exploration of the entire range of music of the western world. Adequate library facilities are also an indispensable adjunct of the Literature and Materials of Music program. In our own instance, we owe a great debt to Isabel Marting, Juilliard Librarian, and her staff, for the splendid manner in which the wide variety of published and recorded materials has been made available.

The selection of repertory, not only for instruction but also for public performance, is of the utmost importance for an educational institution. This selection should not reflect any narrow esthetic allegiance. In order to ensure catholicity of representation, the Administration at

Juilliard does not, except infrequently, choose the actual works to be performed, but is guided by the Faculty. The Administration collates the programs that have been submitted in the spring for performance the following year in order to evaluate them as an entity. On the basis of this evaluation, adjustments are made to ensure a balanced weight of esthetic representation. To be sure, justification of this balance does remain largely a subjective matter, but the self-imposed desire for broad representation is an effective determinant. In a musical society like ours, where so much emphasis is given to virtuosity of performance, there is special need for a school to emphasize the importance of the choice of material.

In our view, the music school not only properly *can* but of necessity *must* be in the advance guard as well as in the position of constantly re-evaluating traditional values. If it is not in the vanguard, it cannot be aware of contemporary developments. And if it is not re-examining values of the past, it is preserving idiosyncrasy of interpretation rather than the tradition of a given esthetic. The young musician should learn that a large part of an enlightened evaluation of any performer's art is determined by the quality of the music he performs and that selection of repertory is a revealing indication of the service he does or does not render the art of music.

In a school of music devoted to these ideals there is not only the opportunity but the need for an awareness on the part of the student of the principles by which he is being taught. The student is aware because the materials of his education are constantly being adjusted to his own state of advancement and abilities, instead of being imposed *a priori*. It is precisely because the serving of this educational ideal makes for a close student-teacher relationship that the Literature and Materials of Music Department inaugurated several years ago a program for the training of teachers. A few of the most gifted students are chosen each year by the Faculty to serve as teaching fellows. Several of this group have gone on to begin their teaching careers in other institutions. It is clear to all of us that this kind of apprenticeship is as effective now as it was in the days of the guilds. In fact, we are so pleased with the splendid achievements of our neophyte teachers in the Literature and Materials of Music Department that we expect to undertake the same kind of teacher-training program with our artist-teachers of the performing skills. Two of the most heartening aspects of our educational program are the manner in which our best students have embraced our program of teaching and the knowledge that a fair percentage of them will develop into highly skilled teachers themselves, capable of giving instruction in music on this level.

It might appear to some that a professional education which considers each student subjectively as well as objectively confuses standards. Let me say again that despite our recognition of subjective differences in talent and goals, we maintain rigid basic objective requirements for those skills and areas of knowledge which we consider essential for any musician. A student who, after a reasonable time in the School, does not give promise of meeting these objective requirements is not continued on the rolls. It is also easy to conclude that a program of education that emphasizes the dynamic and changing nature of the art of music, the importance of exploration, the speciousness of final "rules," and the opposition to absolutism lacks a sense of permanent values. On the contrary, we are convinced that the values inherent in our approach to music education not only are permanent and absolute, but, in fact, parallel those values idealized by a free society which center on the obligation of free men to enlightenment and truth.

Collectively, the musicians of a given epoch have the responsibility for the music of their time. We consider that our portion of this responsibility concerns itself with making sure that students of the art are made aware of music's vast treasure, past and present; making sure that no music is denied them through prejudice—esthetic, political, economic, or social; that they have full "freedom to hear." It is, furthermore, our responsibility to help the student see the music of any given period in the light of its own social, political, and cultural climate; to understand that the esthetic laws and technical considerations of one period cannot be superimposed upon another; to make known to the student the varying convictions of leading musicians, both past and present, in order to help him make his own judgments; to learn that art is not concerned with conformity; to equip the student to deal with the novel without ridicule or fear of its strangeness, yet without being impressed by sheer novelty, and with the ability to probe the depths of the unfamiliar.

Teaching dedicated to these ideals helps the young musician to form the habit of assuming responsibility for the continuation of his own learning. If the student truly absorbs the concept of free inquiry in the field of music, unimpeded by blind adherence to doctrine and tradition, he will bring something of this approach not only to other fields of knowledge but to the conduct of his daily life. Since a free society can grow only through the process of free inquiry by its citizens, it is my profound hope that the basic attitudes instilled through the Literature and Materials program will lead to the maturity of the musician and help toward his enlightenment as a citizen in a democracy. That is the essential idea with which this report is concerned and with which it deals in one particular field of education.

New Rochelle, New York
August 12, 1953

THE

JUILLIARD REPORT
on Teaching the Literature
and Materials of Music

PART I

---◆---

Principles and Aims of the L & M Curriculum

THE SUBSTITUTION of a curriculum in the Literature and Materials of Music for the conventional courses in "music theory," effected at the Juilliard School of Music at the beginning of the academic year 1947–1948, has aroused considerable interest and speculation throughout the musical world. Distinguished teachers and administrators have visited the school to observe classes in the Literature and Materials of Music at first hand, and the school has received a steadily increasing number of written inquiries requesting detailed information concerning the actual operation of the curriculum. It is the purpose of this report to acknowledge this widespread interest by an account of the curriculum from the viewpoint of the faculty that has been involved in its application and development.

The Literature and Materials curriculum (henceforth referred to as "L & M") is described briefly in the current (1952–1953) Juilliard catalogue as follows:

The study of the Literature and Materials of Music constitutes, with study of the major instruments and participation in performance groups (orchestra, chorus, and chamber ensembles), a third principal area of concentration. Each student will be assigned to work with a member of the Literature and Materials faculty, who will be responsible for the instruction of the student in all branches of musical art and technique not specifically in the provinces of the other faculties.

Study of the Literature and Materials of Music is based on music itself, from the Middle Ages to the present day, with emphasis on changing concepts of music in writing and performance. The work done ranges, according to the student's needs, progress, and potentialities, from the rudiments of musical craft to advanced instruction in the techniques of composition, and is accomplished through classroom and individual instruction, discussion groups and seminars, at the discretion of the instructor. The curriculum includes study and analysis of repertoire, development of writing and listening skills, reading assignments, music history, and integrated work adequate to the individual student's needs in such studies as orchestration, basic elements of conducting, keyboard harmony, sight-reading and sight-singing, elementary ensemble performance, and others. Students requiring specialized work in a given area may be assigned to special courses or to other departmental personnel upon recommendation of the instructor.

A block of time, averaging fifteen hours per week, is set aside in each student's schedule for studies in the Literature and Materials of Music. The student is required, within this reserved time, to attend classes or individual lessons, to prepare ensemble performances, or to work at specified assignments at the discretion of the instructor. The Literature and Materials instructor serves as the student's general adviser and plans the student's course of study with a view to facilitating the student's musical development in a well-rounded manner. The student is expected to progress according to his abilities and application, and not mechanically on a year-to-year basis from one course to another.

Qualification in the Literature and Materials of Music is required for graduation in both degree and diploma courses. Recommendation of the instructor must be obtained before the student becomes eligible to take the oral examination for graduation given by a jury of the Literature and Materials faculty In general, four years of study will be required in order to graduate; in some cases, students may qualify in a shorter time, while in others an additional year may prove to be necessary. No student will be considered qualified for graduation on the exclusive basis of a given number of years completed.

In order to satisfy the requirements for graduation in the Literature and Materials of Music, the student will be expected to have gained from his study a wide knowledge of musical literature (repertoire) of his own and other instruments; to give evidence of ability to study new music without the aid of a teacher; to show proficiency in those areas of writing technique conventionally classified as harmony and counterpoint; to read or sing at sight with fluency; to demonstrate familiarity with musical idioms and forms from early times to the present day; in short, to deal with the esthetic and technical complexities of musical art in an independent and intelligent manner. It is finally expected that the student will demonstrate in a satisfactory manner the application of those skills acquired through the Literature and Materials curriculum to the art of musical performance.

This statement gives a concise idea of what we have been attempting to accomplish, and defines the relation of L & M to the over-all program of studies pursued at the Juilliard School. The primary aims of the L & M curriculum may be stated rather simply: to help train gifted students in all branches of the art of music, to encompass a practical understanding of the historical and artistic range of musical creativeness, and to achieve a meaningful transfer of theoretical knowledge into actual performance. This report will attempt to describe in detail all aspects of the curriculum and to explain our continuing belief in the logic and effectiveness of L & M as a means of realizing the aims given.

Anyone seeking an "L & M Method" will be disappointed. The essence of L & M is that it is fluid and that its teaching techniques cannot be prescribed. In the same way as good private teaching, it depends for its success not on the security of a syllabus but on the resourcefulness of the individual teacher, on his imagination, his experience, and his active involvement with music. These living factors do not lend themselves well to systematization. Nothing would be simpler than to say that the Juilliard School of Music had evolved a new "method" or "system" of teaching theory, and nothing would be further from the truth.

The functioning of the L & M curriculum is therefore both more and less complex than may appear at first impression.* It depends first of all upon the special nature of the institution in which it is applied and secondly upon a concept of education that is shared by all teaching participants, by the administrative officers of the school, and ultimately by the students themselves. This concept, or

---

* Details of organization and administration of the curriculum may not be of equal interest to all readers and are, therefore, presented separately in Appendix 1.

"philosophy," of education goes far beyond the boundaries of education in music alone and is not, we feel, applicable only to the music school. Although Juilliard is a special case in some respects, it is actually so only in the sense that every institution has its own characteristics, associations, and traditions. We feel that what we believe about the study of music is not limited in its applicability to the institution with which we have been associated, and although we disclaim any desire of proselytizing, we feel that the approach we have evolved can have many positive suggestions for liberal arts colleges and other institutions in which the study of music is seriously pursued.

The student entering Juilliard is, as a rule, primarily interested in the acquisition of professional skill as a performer or composer. The student and the school both consider that the principal study is, therefore, that involving or leading to mastery of the piano, violin, clarinet, or other chosen field. It goes without saying that the student is expected to work hard and to maintain a high standard of progress and achievement. This is equally true in the second principal area of applied study, that involving pre-professional training in instrumental or vocal ensemble performance. It is the third area of concentration, the L & M curriculum, and its relation to the first two, that concern us here. The relation is direct and constant; since, in effect, L & M is directed toward a goal of musicianship expressed in performance, it necessarily supplements the work of the major teacher. It is of course true that the best major teachers have always been concerned with musical questions beyond fingerings and other matters of pure technique, and that with such teachers the student will derive genuine insight into the relationship between the materials of music and performance. Yet no one questions the necessity or advantage of further serious application by the student to those aspects of musical art or knowledge that traditionally have been explored in theory and history courses. It is the relation of such courses to "applied" music that has not always been clear; indeed, at times there has seemed to be little evidence of any relation whatsoever. "Theory" has tended to become an end in itself (and sometimes a bore to the student), with no explicit or implicit objectives beyond the completion of large numbers of graded exercises. To be sure, it has been intended as part of a training in general musicianship, but it has tended toward an unhealthy and useless isolation. We believe that "theory" as such is important only as it subserves the creative activities of composition and performance, and, to some extent also, the profoundest pleasures of listening to music.

It may be granted that this is not in itself a new concept, nor are the envisaged ends without precedent. We believe, however, that the heretofore conventionally utilized means of realizing these ends have often defeated themselves through arbitrary separations of what has been called "theory" or "history" from performance practices and study of the vast repertoire of music itself, and that the training of the sensibilities, which is the most important element of education in the arts, has been often overlooked.

It was with a view to reaffirming the unity and purpose of "theoretical" and "applied" studies that the L & M curriculum was developed. It is based on the propositions that:

1. the study of music is essentially indivisible; division of theory courses into "Harmony," "Counterpoint," "Form and Analysis," "History," "Orchestration," and other subjects is arbitrary and possibly mechanical;

2. the musical performer will benefit *in his performance* by the most comprehensive understanding of all aspects of music possible and through the realization of the dynamic and changing nature of musical materials and techniques;

3. music is never static, either emotionally or technically: (*a*) "old" music cannot be approached merely as history; (*b*) a static approach to "standard" repertoire indicates the death of a tradition rather than its healthy continuation; (*c*) it is necessary to understand, and to be a part of, the present day; and (*d*) an understanding of the present is necessary in order to understand and evaluate the past, just as an understanding of the past is needed to understand the present;

4. knowledge and direct experience are valuable not so much in themselves as for providing the means of developing sensibility and taste, for acquiring the desire of further knowledge, and for making possible the deepening and sharing of experience in art;

5. one learns one work not only for itself, but in order to

understand other works; one proceeds not only from the general (theory) to the particular (the work), but from the particular to the general (principles);

6. the composer's viewpoint is a necessary and useful supplement to the performer's; the imagination of music (composition) and the re-creation of music (performance) are in fact inseparable.

Based on these beliefs, the L & M curriculum is therefore intended to provide a completely integrated approach to the problems of music as it is practiced in the present and in terms of the technical and esthetic traditions of the past. It is not simply another "theory" curriculum. Theoretical formulations—rules, procedures, methods—are construed as entirely dependent on the changing and living manifestations of musical creativity and are viewed as secondary to direct and varied experience with music itself. We consider that the object of all studies that may be described as "theoretical" is not an ability to overcome the problems posed by abstract exercises but an ability to translate written notes into live music with intelligence, facility, and discrimination.

To do this, it is necessary that the student be very much at home in dealing with a variety of idioms, each involving a concept of melody, a practice of harmony or counterpoint, each relying on certain conventions of precedent and usage, and each differing in some ways from other manners of practice. It is undoubtedly necessary that the student perceive both the continuity and the variety of these manners and practices, that he appreciate styles, techniques, and history as interrelated, and that he also understand relationships among elements of music. Harmony and rhythm, counterpoint and phrase are, for example, relationships that cannot be severed in a musical context. It is desirable that the student, instead of mastering the "rules" of any more or less traditional harmony, understand the functional nature and organic coherence of harmony itself in its relations to rhythm and form. In other words, rather than insist on the rote learning of "rules" covering specific applications of given elements of music, we expect the student to acquire a sound understanding of the nature and relation of those elements in the context of music itself. It follows that the student will in this way also acquire an intelligent perspective on the very "rules" themselves and an ability to manipulate materials in terms of such "rules" as he will be able to formulate for himself on the basis of their applicability in any given instance.

As far as possible, we return to the basic concept that theory *follows* practice and that whereas theoretical formulations may have a convenience and a pedagogic utility, it is nevertheless better, where possible, to attempt direct examination of the realities behind the theoretical abstractions. In a sense, we attempt to retrace the evolution of pedagogic methods and precepts instead of accepting these latter as facts or even as workable aids to learning or teaching. Most important, we constantly want to know what the student is learning, and why; the end we most wish to avoid is a mastery of, let us say, the usual species counterpoint, *if* this implies little beyond an ability to construct passable exercises. On the basis of actual experience, we are compelled to recognize that conventional studies in "theory" too often produce just that result. We believe, having seen many examples, that any student, even the most unmusical, can be *drilled* to write "correct" counterpoint, to "recognize" themes, or to "identify" chords. And while granting the desirability of the student's being able to do these things, we nevertheless maintain that drill does not necessarily lead to understanding and that the results of drilling are valueless unless they assume a place in the workings of an active mind.

The distaste for authorized or required textbooks (or methods), which is generally shared by the L & M faculty, is a natural corollary of that faculty's views on the aims and means of teaching. It does not imply that there are not useful books or helpful methods but simply that no one or more of these is either definitive or universally appropriate. The standard textbooks on counterpoint, for example, beginning with Fux, all claim to base their precepts on some past musical usage, principally Palestrina or Bach. One does not have to go through Fux, Kitson, Richardson, Koechlin, Prout, Goetschius, Wedge, Jeppesen, and a host of others to make a compilation of the ways they differ among themselves as to "rules" and as to what is "correct." But one can examine a variety of works by sixteenth and eighteenth century composers and get an insight into the kinds of practice that these theorists have wished to formulate. With a little diligence, and especially with a little thought, the student should be able to make an equally good formulation; and with a little practice, he should be able to write "exercises," or trial pieces, within any limitations that make stylistic sense.

The Juilliard student is, in other words, expected to acquire specific skills of the sort that conventional theory understands. He is *not* expected, however, to acquire classroom skills that have no meaning or application outside the classroom. He should be able, we feel, to write counterpoint following *any* rules that are given, whether they are dictated by the teacher, copied from a textbook, or derived from an intensive study, on paper and in performance, of contrapuntal music. But at the same time, he should be able to give this proof of skill without believing that such rules or techniques are an end in themselves, that they have any fixed existence, or that they represent any exclusive musical truth.

Before the student has progressed very far in L & M, we hope to have started him toward a thorough and practical knowledge of the mechanics of music, developed his sensitivity in the perception and manipulation of pitch and rhythm, introduced him to the ideas of the evolution of tonality, the devices of composition, the evolution of forms. More, we hope to have broadened his understanding esthetically and helped him to perceive relationships and to get "underneath the notes." We hope to impress upon him that written music is a combination of symbols, that he must understand these symbols and what they express, so that as a performer he can interpret their meanings. We hope to impress upon the student that the study of the mechanics of music has little value unless it is used as a tool, as a means toward dealing with the expressive content of musical art.

One of the questions most frequently raised by those seeking information about the Juilliard curriculum concerns the matter of specific skills. We expect that the student qualifying for the Juilliard degree or diploma will have at the very least a mastery of the "skills" in question equal to that shown by graduates of institutions offering a conventional curriculum in theoretical subjects. If "strict" counterpoint is in question, we expect our students to be able to pass an examination of the usual sort. But in our view, the important things are in what we expect of the student *beyond* that. We want our students to *hear consciously*, to be "virtuoso listeners." An ability to hear component parts, or elements, of the language of music (progressions, intervals, rhythmic patterns, inner textures, instrumental timbres) does not *ipso facto* mean integrated understanding of the sort that can be achieved only when the whole work is clearly perceived as the sum of these parts.

We do not discourage any kind of skill, but we do have some reservations as to what skills are worth acquiring and in what contexts and for what ends. We are dubious about arbitrary means of measuring the value of the skill acquired or of mistaking its quantity for its quality or value. The important thing, again, is the proven or potential applicability of any skill by a conscious person toward a morally justified end, artistic or practical. We feel that skill entails responsibility, even if it is "only" artistic responsibility.

We hope that four years of L & M is enough. It *is* enough if we have persuaded the student that at the end of four years he is prepared for further study of music. It is *not* enough if the student feels that he has completed his studies, with a degree or diploma to prove it. One of the failures of conventional theory (and, in fact, of much that passes for education) is implied in the idea that courses are of given length and that passing them constitutes a lasting accomplishment. We do not see why the music student should "take" two years of harmony, one year of counterpoint, another year of this and another of that; boundaries of this sort encompass either too little or too much. We do not believe that two years, or four years, or twelve years, of, for example, harmony, are enough. Limits to learning are arbitrary, and the arbitrariness increases with the division of learning into "subjects" and "years." We feel that it is important that our students learn that learning is continuous and that the satisfactory completion of any curriculum should not constitute any break in the process.

L & M is successful if it conveys this idea to the student in the field of music and gives him not only means but desire to go on. The student is expected to work at all times to the topmost limits of his capacity. No student graduates merely because he has attended classes for four years; he must have the recommendation of his L & M instructor that he is ready for graduation even before he is allowed to appear for examination.

With our view of continuous and related learning, we can make up examinations only on the basis of the minimum that we will accept at a given stage of the student's development. The best example of what we propose as a *minimum* goal in L & M is provided by an outline of the graduation examination which all candidates for degree or diploma are required to pass. We do not give grades on this examination; the student is judged either *Qualified* or *Not Qualified*. Written comments by the juries provide detailed information on the student's level of attainment. The fact that the examination is conducted by a jury, and is oral, leaves some desirable margin for subjective evaluation and for suiting the content of the examination to the student's major interest. The 1953 outline follows.

GRADUATION EXAMINATION IN THE LITERATURE AND MATERIALS OF MUSIC (GENERAL REQUIREMENTS)

1. This is an *oral* examination, given by a jury of the L & M faculty. It will be of sufficient length and inclusiveness to satisfy the jury completely and unreservedly of the candidate's qualifications for graduation. It will cover every aspect of L & M, with emphasis on such part or parts of the course of study as may seem to the jury most relevant to the individual candidate. In this way, differentiations among standards for singers, composers, pianists, etc., may be made directly by the L & M faculty as each case presents itself.

2. The examining jury will be given beforehand the "dossier" or running file covering the candidate's work with his major L & M teacher. This dossier * will inform the jury extensively about the candidate's background and give specific information about works studied, skills acquired, attitudes, etc., from the viewpoint of his L & M teacher.

The jury will furthermore have, attached to the "dossier," examples of the student's written work throughout the period of his enrollment. This written work must demonstrate as a *minimum*:

(A) Reasonable proficiency in the procedures of conventional counterpoint and traditional harmony.

(B) Ability to notate music legibly and intelligently.

(C) Ability to write an original "assignment" that,

* See Part III, page 59 below.

even if it does not show creative originality, at least demonstrates musical thinking.

3. After examining the student's written work, the jury will require the student to read at sight, on his own instrument, a work or part of a work, to be selected by the jury. The student may be asked to discuss his impressions of the work and the manner in which he believes that he addresses himself to its problems. The student may be asked further to discuss the manner in which he studies new works.

4. The student will be required to demonstrate to the jury's satisfaction some degree of skill at the keyboard. Demonstrations may or may not include such aspects of keyboard study as playing a four-part chorale, realizing a simple figured bass, reading from an open score, improvising freely or on a given subject, transposing at sight, etc. It is to be expected that requirements as to proficiency will differ for pianists, conductors, and composers on the one hand, and for singers and players of orchestral instruments on the other.

5. The student will be required to answer questions on a variety of subjects. The jury may ask questions covering the following areas:

(A) Knowledge of instruments: ranges, uses, characteristics, etc.

(B) Music history. Accurate, and not vague, information will be expected on all periods (within reasonable limits).

(C) Technical terms. The student's knowledge is to be tested extensively. He must in all cases go beyond mere "definition" of, for example, "Italian Sixth," and must show how, why, when, where it may be or has been used.

(D) Basic conducting techniques, with emphasis on ability to read a page of music in score (flexible standards for different classes of students).

(E) Knowledge of repertoire. The student will be ex-

pected to show a respectable knowledge of repertoires of his own and other instruments, standard
orchestral works, operas, etc. He will be expected
to sing or play melodies or subjects from these
repertoires at the request of the jury.

(F) Style and criticism. The jury will attempt to pose
questions that will show the student's degree of
ability to evaluate performance and authenticity
of detail.

(G) The student will be required to satisfy the jury as
to his ability to sing at sight.

6. The L & M examining jury may require the candidate
for graduation to discuss analytically (technically, esthetically, historically, etc.) one or more of the works which the
student has chosen for his graduation examination in his major instrument.

A sample of such an examination, as actually applied,
will be found in Appendix 4.

In the following pages, we shall attempt to show in specific detail how instruction in L & M is designed to prepare the student for this type of comprehensive examination. It should be borne in mind that this examination
constitutes an inquiry into the student's attainment of a
number of more or less demonstrable skills and qualifications. No examination can be devised that will weigh or
evaluate intangibles, but the latitude accorded the jury
affords it the opportunity of judging how far beyond the
minimum standards the student has progressed and how
well the student is able to function as a mature and conscious musician.

PART II

---◆·◆---

The Entering Student: Basic Vocabulary and Basic Attitude

THE VARIATION in background among students entering Juilliard is enormous and involves not only great differences in natural endowment but all shadings of general culture from relatively high sophistication to the lowest passable standard set by our secondary schools. The musical training, experience, and development of these entrants also show wide disparities, since, while many entrants are excellently prepared in terms of theoretical background, other students may be admitted who give evidence of latent, though uncultivated, talent, or who have reached an advanced level of technical performing skill without any comprehension of many basic musical materials. The latter case is particularly frequent among students admitted as singers. It is not unusual to find a singer, endowed by nature with an exceptional voice, who is ill at ease with written notes, who cannot sing at sight the simplest diatonic melody, and who cannot tell one orchestral instrument from another. The Juilliard School is prepared to admit students with marked aptitude for performance but with no technical theoretical preparation.

Although most entering students are high school graduates, the entering group is less homogeneous in culture than, for example, a group entering a liberal arts college. Juilliard students come not only from many sections of the United States but from many foreign countries as well, and they represent almost all economic and social strata. In addition, there is apt to be a somewhat wider variation in age among entering students at Juilliard, since a number of applicants may have engaged in professional or semi-professional work for some years before deciding to continue study. These factors tend to make an entering "class" at Juilliard rather heterogeneous, and it cannot be said that a cohesive element is always provided by any common goal or interest in musical study. The aims of Juilliard students differ considerably, and their attitudes toward music seem at times highly specialized.

Juilliard also admits each year, as "new" students, a fairly large number of students who have completed one or more years of study at other institutions, here or abroad, on the college or conservatory level. There is also, in each entering group, a representation of students who have attended classes at the Juilliard Preparatory Division or at secondary schools such as New York's High School of Music and Art, or who have had better than average preparation in aspects of music beyond performance techniques. Students in these categories are often ready for intermediate or advanced study, though not necessarily so.

It is the responsibility of the L & M faculty to determine exactly where each student must begin and how to plan a curriculum for each student, considered as an individual. Juilliard has no "freshman class," or formally established first-, second-, or third-year courses of study. Since, in principle, there are not even formally organized classes (of harmony, counterpoint, rudiments of music, etc.), the entering student cannot simply be assigned to specified courses. His career as a student at Juilliard (in everything that does not concern his major lessons or his performing assignments in orchestra, chorus, or chamber music) begins with an interview with a member of the L & M faculty. The instructor attempts to evaluate the student's level of general musicianship, to test his ear, to discover the amount and effectiveness of his previous training, to make notes on his attitude toward his work, to inquire about the kind of music the student has played, heard, and enjoyed; also to gauge the student's general intelligence and probable aptitude in learning, to inquire as to the student's experience in performing as a soloist, in ensembles, orchestras, or bands; and finally, to elicit an expression of the student's interests and aims. In short, the interviewer attempts to get as reasonably well-rounded a picture of the student as is possible during a single introductory interview. The information and impressions gathered by the instructor (and these impressions, it is clearly understood, are not taken as a final word) are tabulated on a card, which is passed on to the L & M instructor to whom the student is eventually assigned. This card becomes the first item in the comprehensive "dossier" which will record the student's work and progress from entrance through graduation. A reproduction of such a card, filled out for a fictitious "average" student, is given as Figure 1.

The "average" student is of course non-existent, and it is difficult even to attempt the formulation of a composite sketch. Nevertheless, it is possible to suggest some phenomena that recur frequently enough to tend to delineate a "middle ground." On the basis of several years of giving entrance tests and interviews, and of introducing new students into L & M studies, we feel that we can make the following general statements about "The Entering Student":

1. He (or she) is between seventeen and nineteen years of age and has received a high school education or the equivalent.
2. He is accustomed to "authoritarian" teaching and has little or no conception of *learning* (finding out), as opposed to *being taught*.
3. He has attained skill in singing or playing an instrument (this, of course, being necessary for admission) but does not have a very developed interest in anything musical beyond technical mastery of this instrument. The interest is often a "trade" interest, focused on the hope of earning a living through the instrument.
4. He is apt to be very diligent, even single-minded, about working at his major instrument, but he often has little knowledge of musical repertoire beyond what he has been taught. His curiosity about repertoire (except for students majoring in conducting or composition) is as a rule very limited.

JUILLIARD SCHOOL OF MUSIC
Literature and Materials of Music Interview

Name: X ......

Major: Piano

Course of Study Requested: B. S.

Date of Birth: July 4ᵗʰ 1936

1. Background of Candidate (Theory etc.):
8 years of private study, (piano)
1 year high school music appreciation.
Rudimentary harmony (piano teacher)

2. Experience (Listening and Performing):
Has sung 2 years in church choir.
Some accompanying (high school glee club)
Solo performances for school assembly.
Has listened to NBC & N.Y. Philharmonic
broadcasts. Records.

3. Estimate of Candidate:
A. General Intelligence. appears. average.
B. Ear. fair. but. untrained.
C. Aptitude shows quick response to untrained questions.
D. Attitude seems very sure of himself.
E. Other.
Shows symptoms of musical.
antipathy. toward early classical music.
and general ear training.

4. Basic Vocabulary. ok. except for clefs, chords
and general ear training.

5. Comments:
This boy has had very little
musical training, but does not know
it. Check with major teacher
on pianistic ability. Seems to
have a great deal of drive
and confidence. Does not
think Mozart very interesting.
"Played one as a beginner."
Prefers "modern music," i.e.
Kabalevsky (sonatina), Rachmaninoff
(piano concertos), De Falla
(Ritual Fire Dance).

(Instructor C)
Signature of Interviewer

F. 169-1M-5-52

Figure 1. Reproduction of Interview Card, Filled out as Sample

47

5. He has, if he is a string or wind instrument player, participated in high school orchestras or bands but has seldom been given either opportunity or encouragement to participate in chamber music or ensembles.

6. He has, if a pianist, played almost no chamber music but has done a little "accompanying."

7. He has heard very little first-rate "live" music but has done desultory and haphazard listening to records and radio. His musical taste is apt to be formed by the repertoire of the high school band, or by the culture diffused by simplified "music appreciation" courses, or by major network broadcasting. His judgments are often made on the basis of a vague emotional stimulus.

8. He is more interested in virtuoso performance and in performers than in what is performed.

9. He has an untrained ear. In most cases, no attempt has been made to train the ear.

10. Perhaps most important, he has not had music in his home and has never felt it as an intimate and vital part of his environment.

If these conclusions seem on the whole rather negative and unpromising, it should be pointed out at once that by far the greater number of students respond very quickly to a new kind of stimulation and environment. Yet these conclusions about the entering student cannot be dismissed lightly; they point to several curious things about musical culture in America at mid-century and reflect directly on the nature of education in many of our secondary schools. Since these things affect very markedly what we are trying to do at Juilliard, passing attention must be given them in connection with this report.

To a number of entering students, the idea of L & M comes as a shock for which they are unprepared intellectually, musically, and temperamentally. It is a fundamental task of the L & M faculty to help these students make a transition and an adjustment to a new idea of learning and to persuade many of them to think, for the first time, of an *art* of music that is larger and more enduring than their own interests in it. Nearly every member of the L & M faculty has felt the necessity of devoting considerable time with entering students to clarification of the purposes of the curriculum and to explaining not so much the nature of what the student may expect to *receive* as what he will be expected to give, or find within himself. The reorientation of some students is not easy, and in many cases it requires both time and patience. One of the most interesting obstacles is language. A high school diploma is no longer assurance that the student can understand English or express himself coherently. Perhaps unfortunately, the written and spoken words remain our most effective media of communication, even in teaching music. Although L & M cannot solve the difficulties posed in this respect, many members of the faculty have been highly conscious of the problem and have noted it in reports. It remains essential for the success of L & M teaching that the student understand, intellectually, at least the basic "philosophy" of the curriculum. The student must be made to feel that he is a participant, rather than merely an object of instruction.

Many of our entering students have been treated too long as children, with the result, in some cases, that capacities, skills, and energies have lain dormant. The student who has been "told" everything is apt to be inhibited and unwilling to trust his instincts, tastes, or judgments. A report of one L & M instructor points out: "It took at least a month to overcome the perfectly terrifying inhibitions of the students in expressing themselves, either by speech, or playing, or composing. They are afraid of being pounced upon and of doing the wrong thing." For such a student, everything is apt to be black or white: there must be a "correct" way of doing anything (i.e., the way his most recent teacher has told him to do it), all other ways being "wrong." This is also the student for whom contemporary music is apt to be "weird," a characterization that crops up with some frequency during entrance interviews. A very curious phenomenon is observable with this type of student: he is slavish in attempting to follow directions, markings, or suggestions, but at the same time is more than normally inaccurate in doing so.

The problems posed by language and by the patterns of authoritarian teaching are not confined to the music school. They affect us as they affect any institution in which an ideal of education is seriously pursued. Some of the phenomena noted above are, however, of unique concern to the music school. This is not the place for a full discussion of problems in American musical culture that are far from being resolved. No one, however, will question that the great increase in quantity of music brought about by radio and recordings, and the great increase of organized musical activity in the high schools, have had marked effects. In a sense, these effects have been contradictory: the professional has been brought into the home, while the amateur has been taken out of it. The radio, whatever its positive contributions, has encouraged stereotyped "music appreciation" and the deadliest kind of passive listening, while musical activity in the high school, for all its remarkable accomplishments in recent years, occasionally seems directed more toward a self-perpetuating music-education program than toward the values of music itself. The attitudes that these phenomena engender influence the student's thinking more than superficially and tend to widen very greatly the unfortunate gap between active performer and passive audience. What the student in many cases needs is to rediscover the sense of intimate participation and of deeply satisfying personal meaning and communication that music affords.

Whatever the student's background and ability may be, the instructor, during the first weeks of acquaintance with the student, is expected to find out a good deal about him beyond such information as has been furnished by the entrance interview. The preparation of many entrants is, of course, found to be greatly superior to the average, in terms both of techniques and of attitude toward study. In all cases, the instructor must plan work for which the student is ready; he will not, as a rule, find that he has a homogeneous class.

Every student entering the school is tested on what we have termed "Basic Vocabulary." We are agreed that there are certain basic skills, as well as terms and symbols, that are as necessary to the understanding of music as the knowledge of the multiplication table is to the working of all mathematics. Thorough knowledge of these terms and acquisition of these skills to a usable degree must be accomplished before the student goes on to what we consider the effective study of music. As basic material we propose that the student:

1. Recognize that there are symbols and names of fundamental pitch and time ideas:

   (*a*) Names of linear organizations: intervals, modes, scales (of all types)
   (*b*) Names of vertical organizations: intervals, triads, and other chords
   (*c*) Names of time organizations: tempo, meter, pulse;

2. Recognize that certain basic skills must be practiced so that they are available for effective use. These include hearing, reading, writing, singing, and playing all of the above.
3. Begin to acquire facility in the following:

   (*a*) Transposition
   (*b*) Reading of clefs
   (*c*) Recognition and use of instruments
   (*d*) Reading from score.

As a check on the above, the following examination in "Basic Vocabulary" is given each entrant during the first week or two of the academic year.

TEST OF BASIC VOCABULARY

Student must rate 90 percent or better before becoming eligible to proceed with any further instruction in L & M. A student who cannot pass this test at the end of the first year will be placed on probation.

1. Student must be able to write, play, sing, and identify by ear and eye the following:

   (a) Major scale
   (b) Minor scale (all forms: harmonic, melodic, natural)
   (c) Chromatic scale
   (d) Pentatonic scale(s)
   (e) Whole-tone scale
   (f) Modes

2. Student must recognize all key signatures.
3. Student must read with facility in G treble clef and F bass clef and be familiar with C alto and C tenor.
4. Student must be able to recognize and play or sing accurately metrical patterns written in all time signatures.
5. Student must be able to read, hear, and reproduce all intervals between two pitches (within the compass of an octave) sounded successively or simultaneously.
6. Student must identify without hesitation:

   (a) Major triad (all positions)
   (b) Minor triad (all positions)
   (c) Augmented triad
   (d) Diminished triad
   (e) Dominant seventh chord (all inversions)
   (f) Chords built on seconds or fourths

7. Student must have a basic understanding of the characteristics of instruments used in standard orchestral literature.
8. Student must be familiar with the most common foreign terms governing tempo and expression.

To attain the required grade of 90 percent or better on this test, the student of average preparation needs to spend the equivalent of a semester. A few students are found to be qualified on entrance, while some late-starters, especially voice students, may require up to a full year of work.

In stating, as above, that we propose that the student recognize that certain basic skills must be practiced, we touch upon a fundamental pedagogic concept in L & M, and one that involves "basic attitude" as well as basic vocabulary. It is the recognition of the need for practice that is eventually as important as the practice itself. The greater part of the responsibility falls where it rightly should: *on the student.* He is expected to spend at least an hour a day developing these skills outside the classroom and away from the supervision of a teacher. Classroom drill is effective up to a point, but the desire to improve techniques and sharpen skills must be kindled within each student to the point at which an inner discipline of learning is acquired. Such a discipline is the one that is lastingly effective and personally meaningful; its attainment marks one of the stages in the progress of the unformed student toward becoming a mature and responsible person and musician. It is, in a sense, the first mark of the potential growth and development that is one of the definable goals of education.

It is natural that instructors will differ in their ways and means of helping and persuading their students, especially in the early stages, toward this goal. Here personalities must, and should, enter. We allow for the possibility of temperamental incompatibilities between teacher and student by authorizing changes of teacher where change seems likely to be helpful. We do not believe in assigning students in job lots or in considering them as so many subjects to be graded. The relation of the student to his L & M instructor is a four-year one, between individuals, and we believe that everything possible should be done, administratively, to make the relation agreeable to both parties concerned, even at the cost of taking considerable extra time for interviews and adjustments.

Actual instruction in "Basic Vocabulary" may take a variety of forms. The L & M faculty is aware of the danger of divorcing this work from its application in musical examples. The job of learning to recognize intervals quickly and easily may, for example, too simply take the form of constant drill on intervals over a fairly long period. We see the necessity for this, but we feel that we can, in all cases, illustrate material through its *use* in music. And while, in the early stages, identification as such must be emphasized, a leading toward ideas of use and application may be introduced. The student should be made aware of the differences between studying and listening to music, and listening to and identifying *elements* of music. At the beginning, the student should, however, be made conscious of likenesses rather than differences in Western music and should recognize that it is not so much the material that differs as it is the uses to which the material is put.

If this is done, we find that an additional objective can be attained in the first stages of study: we are able to begin overcoming a kind of provincialism in music that is characteristic of many of our entering students. Most of them are aware of only that limited portion of music history and repertoire that is considered, in lay language, "classical," i.e., Bach to Brahms, and the average student's knowledge and curiosity are not what can by any stretch of the imagination be called extensive, even within these limits. But the study of rudiments of pitch and interval may well be linked to a first look at plain chant, and drill on rhythms and notation can be illuminated by examples from Stravinsky or Bartók. Naturally, in the early stages, none of these musical examples can or need be discussed in terms of preference, taste, or value; they are merely shown to *exist*, and the instructor will have suggested that they are not unique, or isolated, or unrelated.

PART III

❮━━━━◆━━━━❯

Teaching of L & M in
the First Two Years

DIRECTLY after his entrance interviews, the student who is accepted for admission is assigned to one of the members of the L & M faculty, who will act as his L & M teacher throughout his career at the school. Assignment is made by the office of the registrar, subject to review by the Chairman of the L & M faculty. The basis of assignment is the student's major study, the object being to assure reasonably balanced performing and study groups in the class of each instructor. Thus, if Instructor A does not have, for example, a clarinetist among his students, one will be assigned to him from the entering class; if Instructors A, B, and C have nine, seven, and four pianists, respectively, an effort will be made to even the totals through the distribution of new students. One of the principal advantages sought in the L & M curriculum is that of performing and reading as much music as possible in class. To that end, it is desirable that the students assigned to each instructor represent a cross-section of performance media and performance skills. Each instructor should have as a minimum within his class a string quartet, several pianists in various stages of advancement, a few singers, and a small group of wind instrument players.

Each instructor is thus responsible for a group that remains of fairly constant size, as graduating students are replaced each year by those entering. At any given time, the instructor should have a group fairly well divided as to levels of advancement, and fairly well distributed as to pianists, other instrumentalists, and singers. In the fluid organization of the daily and hourly program, the instructor may call any or all of these students together as the need may arise. If it is desired to study or perform a work for small orchestra, such an ensemble can be made up within the class. Or, pianists may be assigned to work with chamber music groups; singers may be asked to prepare madrigals; sonatas for various instruments may be performed, as well as duos, trios, quartets, and larger works.

The student devotes not less than eight hours per week (exclusive of homework and outside assignments) to L & M. There is no formula for the utilization of the eight hours; the instructor-adviser may assign classwork or make other dispositions in whatever way he feels will most benefit the student. In general, the student will attend several classes with a Teaching Fellow who assists the instructor. A certain number of hours may or may not be devoted to the preparation of ensemble works for performance and analysis or discussion. In the first years, some attention will usually be given also to review and drill on "basic vocabulary" and to secondary keyboard instruction. All these possibilities, however, are at the discretion of the instructor.

From the instructor's point of view, the first important step of the academic year is to take stock of his returning students, checking their status and progress, and to survey and examine the new students assigned to him. On this basis, the instructor proceeds to organize study groups, conferences, classes, and other work, on the basis of common needs or interests and levels of advancement. Each instructor usually reserves one and one-half hours per week for a meeting of his entire "class." This meeting serves both as a co-ordinating meeting (for announcements, check-ups, etc.) and as an occasion on which all students (from "freshmen" to "seniors") may have a chance to perform for their classmates. Some instructors also use these meetings for general lectures, or for talks by invited guests on specific topics of interest to all the students. A detailed discussion of materials and approaches used in these general meetings will be found in the concluding section of this chapter.

In taking stock of his students and in forming study groups and classes, the instructor uses as a guide for his own information the "dossier," or permanent record and check, which follows the student from entrance to graduation. This "dossier" (we shall refer to it in this way from this point on) is one of the most important innovations of the L & M curriculum. It is reproduced in full (with a sample student's record filled in) as Appendix 2. It serves both as "reminder" to the instructor and as a complete record for the student. This record, along with examples of the student's written work and any other relevant papers, goes to the jury of the L & M faculty that interviews the student ready for graduation.

The use of the "dossier" in the L & M curriculum should not be minimized. It enables the instructor to keep informed about each student's work and is a valuable aid in planning study. It provides a unifying factor governing the areas of study to be covered, while at the same time it does not prescribe either method or chronology of study. Thus, each instructor may adapt the *rate and means* of achieving certain goals to the capacities and interests of different students. It acts as both guide and record, without assuming any feature of a syllabus.

In principle, the entering student is regarded as somewhat of a probationer until he has passed the "Basic Vocabulary Test," * a record of which is required on page two of the student's file, or dossier. In practice, he is admitted to certain classes, including large group meetings (see above), and an attempt is made to orient him for future studies. A constant effort is made to ensure that the concentration on "basic vocabulary" is always linked to musical examples and practices, and at the same time it is hoped that a constructive attitude toward study will have been encouraged. Perhaps the most important element of the beginning student's experience is the fact that he will be constantly exposed to music, in performance and discussion, music of all periods and for all media, and he will be called upon to participate, to the level of his ability, in these performances. He will *immediately* be encouraged to think of music beyond the problems of fingerings, tone production, and technical mastery, and will

* See above, p. 53.

be asked to perceive or consider the relation of whatever technique or whatever theory he has mastered to the whole problem of musical performance, musical coherence, and musical style.

In the beginning, the student will probably be "exposed" to considerable material that is beyond his immediate comprehension or experience. It is hoped, however, that all new experience will be presented in such a way as to whet the student's desire to know more. One of the foundations of what (for want of a better term) we must call "basic attitude" is the notion that the field of music is vast, and that all musical problems are susceptible of many solutions; that one looks not only backward, at tradition, but forward, to the continuation and transformation of tradition. We want the student to know that music is complex, many-sided; that it involves not only techniques, but history, esthetics, and perspectives; and that it is not mastered easily, if at all.

The "average" student, conditioned by a ready-made, cash-and-carry concept of education, wishes to *know*, principally so that he can then *say* that he knows (having taken a course). Unfortunately, most students do not understand that to know is merely the first step in wishing to know more. The "average" student, again, seems to assume that there is a *method* (prescribed, hence necessarily correct and incontrovertible) of learning any subject, just as there is a *date* for the discovery of America. He cherishes the illusion of progress through numbered or graded exercises and is not encouraged to look within himself. The influences of certain "philosophies of education" have also conditioned the student to consider far too much of history and human effort in terms of tendency rather than in terms of value.

These are important negatives in our first encounters with the majority of our students. They are, in a sense, beyond our control, since they stem broadly from our primary and secondary schools, family, environment, and general culture. Our view of education is, in general, opposed to set methods and to disciplines imposed from above. We insist that the student assume a large measure of responsibility for his own education and we consider it our first duty to help him understand the necessity for this. We feel that the teacher can provide tools for exploring, for sharpening perception, for deriving meaning from experience, and for formulating values, but we do not feel that it is the function of the teacher to be the oral equivalent of a textbook.

Music history, into which we plunge our students obliquely, offers an example. We do not, in the accepted sense, teach music history at all. We do, however, range over the history of music by *making* music. At the same time, we try to keep in mind, and to call to the student's attention, certain relatives and certain absolutes. In a fully meaningful view of music of many times and places, it is a mistake to view one phenomenon solely as *tending* toward a more perfected development. Haydn not only leads to Beethoven but is also Haydn. It is evident that each stage of any development gave esthetic satisfaction in its own time and place and that it hence must be viewed as a complete artistic expression with its own techniques and esthetic aims. It is evident that we do not know what the music of the year 2050 will be, but we do not, and must not, view the music of 1950 as an "early stage" of the music of the twenty-first century. We hear it, and value it, as it is offered to us in our time.

The beginning student, then, may hear (or participate in performances of) examples of Western music from plain chant to Schoenberg. We try to make him hear with his own ears. He is apt to be puzzled, hurt, inarticulate. No one has ever before expected so much effort of him. He misses the comforts of being told what to hear and what to think. He is afraid he is not learning anything! But this stage is, with most students, of short duration. The point is usually made: that art is long and various. The student perceives that in music there are "vertical" and "horizontal" combinations and organizations, both in principle and in practice. He learns that he must acquire the ability to recognize and differentiate these and that they are in themselves important only as they subserve the expressive ends of musical art.

In practice, some of these aims may be approached even during the period in which the student is still striving to master the "basic vocabulary." Most progress is, however, made during the first year of studies that we consider as being properly a part of the Literature and Materials curriculum. (This first year would correspond to that portion of the curriculum formerly offered as L & M I.) Actual instruction in the early stages may take almost any number of forms. The members of the L & M faculty are guided by agreement on general goals to be attained at the end of a year's study (for the "average" student, of course), but they are free to choose means of approaching them. Broadly speaking, these goals were defined (at the inception of the L & M program) as follows:

OUTLINE OF SUBJECTS AND TECHNIQUES TO BE COVERED IN THE FIRST YEAR OF L & M

(An introduction to music literature and techniques)

The basic aim of the Literature and Materials curriculum is to give the student an awareness of as many aspects as possible of the art of music and its techniques. The study of any phase (harmony, form, counterpoint, etc.) must be on a basis that is comparative and relative (in terms of historical usages) rather than absolute (in terms of "rules"). The underlying conception of L & M teaching is that the so-called "fields of theoretical study" (harmony, counterpoint, form, and analysis) are in actuality inseparable.

Compositional styles: Students will be expected to recognize and to write melodies and cadences in the styles of various representative composers.

Introduction to types of literature:
Song
Piano
Choral
Chamber music
Orchestral
Opera

Form: Introductory study of one-, two-, and three-part forms; rondo, variation, fugue, and sonata principles.

Scale structures:
Major and minor (key signatures)
Modal
Whole-tone
Pentatonic
Chromatic (twelve-tone)

Rhythm:

    Fundamental rhythmic concepts (metric patterns, time signatures, pulse.)

    Relation of tempo to the expressive and structural elements of music

    Rhythmic organization in terms of length:

        Measure

        Motive

        Phrase

        Short pieces

        Long compositions

    Study of rhythmic devices used in composition

Harmony:

    All triads in all positions

    All seventh chords

    Figured bass principles

    Overtone series

    Cadences

    Use of non-harmonic tones

    Simple melodic harmonization, primarily diatonic but including simple modulation via common chord and common tone

    Sequential harmonic patterns

    Harmonic organization of a phrase (original part writing)

Miscellaneous:

    Relation of words and music

    Recognition of all intervals: melodic and harmonic

    Instrumental sounds, ranges, and usages

    Transposition

It is suggested that each instructor assign a list of thirty works in addition to regular class assignments—material to be drawn from all periods from the twelfth to the twentieth centuries. Students to study these works, via records, sufficiently to be able to recognize them at the end of the year.

This statement of objectives may be compared with a typical final examination given to first-year L & M students:

FIRST-YEAR L & M FINAL EXAMINATION

1. At home: Write a three-minute composition for own instrument (or voice) and two or three others.
2. Short quiz on fundamental technical material:

   (a) Scales; modes
   (b) Song forms
   (c) Transposition of instruments
   (d) Compositional devices (augmentation, inversion, etc.)
   (e) Interval textures
   (f) Harmonic formations (augmented sixths, diminished sevenths, etc.)

3. Dictation:

   (a) Melodic and harmonic intervals
   (b) Simple folk tunes

4. Write three short melodies in differing styles, each for a different instrument.
5. Harmonize two phrases of a Bach chorale melody.
6. Write a piece for B-flat clarinet and snare drum, using rhythmic imitation.
7. In four-part harmony, modulate from C major to C-sharp minor, labeling all ornamental tones contained therein.
8. Records: Identify the period and, if possible, the composer of the following works. (Include Gibbons, Mozart, Lassus, Stravinsky, J. S. Bach, Schumann, Ravel, Beethoven, Schoenberg, Frescobaldi, Bartók, Chopin, Debussy, Brahms, Pachelbel, Byrd, etc.)
9. Five hearings of a short sonata-allegro movement (of

Haydn or Mozart—quartet or symphony). Analyze aurally.

10. *Optional:* Quiz on listening material assignments given during semester.

For the examination above, three two-hour periods are allotted.

REPORTS BY INSTRUCTORS—FIRST YEAR OF COURSE

Perhaps the most interesting aspect of the L & M curriculum for those not familiar with its actual application at Juilliard is that involving the differing approaches used by various instructors. Following are some representative examples, taken from reports made by the instructors themselves:

Instructor A:

My over-all approach was: the dispensation of the broadest historical outline of music, with specific emphasis on melodic characteristics typical of various periods and nationalities and, more generally, on esthetic and idiomatic phenomena in composition. Lectures? Yes, I talked a great deal. Arguing—free-for-all discussions? Indeed! Almost the order of the day. We analyzed selected works by means of records and in live performance. In "lessons" we covered scales, intervals, classic harmony, and form, all these aurally, orally, and in written work. Counterpoint I treated merely as a technique, not handling exercises other than rounds.

I ordered no textbooks to be bought but recommended some to students who specifically wished me to do so. I did cause them to buy folksong collections, Bach Chorales, some orchestral study scores, and other material. Listening to as much "standard" music as possible was required, via records, rehearsals, and concerts.

Strong emphasis on written technical work was a regular feature of the last half of my course. We also did a great deal of "free" composition, none "in the style of," at least not consciously. I made a good deal of sight-singing, individually and in group-form, and of ear-training, idem, both from the angle of interval and chord recognition and of form and style recognition.

Instructor B:

The following is a more or less complete outline of sessions in a first-year class conducted by this instructor.

FIRST THROUGH SIXTH SESSIONS:

    General study of styles of all periods, emphasizing melodic approach

    How "methods" of writing changed

    Study of cadences:

        Palestrina

        Bach

        Nineteenth century

        Twentieth century

    Characteristics of various composers

    Melodic dictation:

        Study of range and curve of melody

        Relation of fundamental beat to melodic rhythm

        Melodies for instruments written and performed

        Specific examples of specific points found in music brought in

        Listening to compositions for melodic form and line

NEXT SIX SESSIONS:

    Study of general harmonic movement:

        Triadic progressions—compare pre-Bach, nineteenth century, twentieth century

        Lead back to modal writing—organum period and twentieth century

Trace two-part counterpoint rhythmically from organum

Rhythmic canons written—wood-block and snare drum

Canons (only one melodic line for voice and hand clapper; play melody and sing rhythm)

Pieces written for instrument and drum (instrument demonstrated)

Back to harmony—some general observations, such as doubling, spacing, etc.

Work covered through first eight weeks:

I. Study of range and curve of melodies
   (*a*) melodies brought in by students and played in class to determine range and curve
   (*b*) short whole-note melodies written by students with definite curve in mind
   (*c*) notes taken on desirability of curve in a melody and possibilities of range

II. Study of fundamental beat in melodies
   (*a*) melodies played on piano by instructor to demonstrate:
      1. accent on fundamental beat
      2. accent not on fundamental beat
   (*b*) melodies written in class to demonstrate accent not on fundamental beat
   (*c*) examples of published melodies brought in by class to demonstrate above
   (*d*) how to accent an off-beat (conclusions from class research)
      1. make note longer
      2. use syncopation
      3. use tied notes
      4. make it the high point
      5. precede by rest.

III. Short study of harmonies and harmonic progressions

(*a*) study of possibilities of harmonic progressions

(*b*) examples of chord progressions in melodies (not original) brought in by students and discussed

(*c*) melodies written by students for voice or an instrument with piano accompaniment

(*d*) records played and chamber works performed by students to determine direction of harmonies

(*e*) examples of melodies (not original) brought in by students with definite harmonic direction indicated (parallel with or contrary to melody)

IV. Early music—pre-Bach

(*a*) examples of early triadic progressions brought in by class

(*b*) observations and notes made on characteristics of early music

    1. pedal point

    2. "thirdless triads" (open fifths)

    3. raised fourth

(*c*) modes

    1. modal melodies written by students for various instruments; played by students and criticized

    2. records played as examples of modal music

(*d*) talk on organum (by student)

    1. three periods explained

    2. historic survey of the period

    3. organum characteristics

V. Canons

(*a*) "dry" canons (percussion only) written and performed in class

(*b*) also voice with percussion; voice with instrument; voices only; instruments only

VI. Study of the trombone

(*a*) range explained, including seven positions and pedal tone

(b) technical possibilities explained by trombone student

(c) mutes demonstrated

(d) study of trombone passages that sound difficult but are relatively easy to play

VII. Rhythm

(a) rhythm values explained and copied

(b) advantages of tied notes explained

(c) examples of interesting rhythms written by students, tapped and sung in class

(d) melodies with contrasting rhythm accompaniments written and performed by students (voice and piano, voice and tapping)

VIII. Melody writing—further study

ways to develop a motive melodically (compositional devices)

1. repetition
2. relative repetition
3. interval expansion
4. interval contraction
5. inversion
6. retrogression
7. diminution
8. augmentation
9. variation
10. dismemberment
11. enlargement
12. imitation

IX. Dictation—occasional dictation given, listening for:

(a) highest and lowest melodic notes (goals)

(b) main rhythmic idea (thematic kernels)

Records played in class (played only in part):

Bach: Brandenburg Concerto (6) II—for chamber orchestra

Bartók: Violin Concerto

Sibelius: Fourth Symphony (second movement)

Shostakovich: Sixth Symphony (first and second movements)

Chavez: Indian Symphony and Violin Sonatina

Gabrieli, Giovanni: Canzona in mixolydian mode

Loeillet: Sonata for Harpsichord and Flute—straight minor with modulations

Italian ballads of the fourteenth century for voice,
viol, and trombone—in Dorian with many "modulations"—played in full (one side)

Pezel, Johann: Suite (for two trumpets, two trom-
bones)—starts in C major, no changes first side;
second side, major scale with leading tone lowered

Bartók: Contrasts for clarinet, piano, and violin—Lo-
crian mode

Barber, Samuel: Capricorn Concerto

Schuman, William: Symphony for Strings

Ninth and tenth weeks: Study and discussion of cadences:
Sixteenth century:
Palestrina motets
Lassus motets

Bach cadences:
Chorales
C Minor Partita (organ)
Cantata, "God's Time Is Best"

Nineteenth century:
Schubert: F Minor Fantasie, Opus 103 (piano, four
hands)
Schumann: Opus 17, Fantasie for Piano
Berlioz: Requiem
Wagner: Faust Overture
Also references to Hungarian folk music and Rich-
ard Strauss

Contemporary cadences:
Ravel: Trio for Violin, Cello, and Piano
Hindemith: Six English Songs
Bartók: Fourth String Quartet
Copland: Music for the Theatre
Schoenberg: Piano Concerto

Aside from class discussions, examples, and analyses, students were required to bring in other examples and reports.

Eleventh through fifteenth weeks:
(*a*) Triads. At this point, a survey of music for mixed

chorus and for string quartet for the purpose of drawing conclusions and making observations on the use of simple triads. Notes made on:

doubling	fifths and octaves
spacing	inversion
voice leading	position
chord progression	harmonic rhythm
seventh chords	cross relation
altered notes	

Among student assignments: to find in published music examples of the following:

Diminished triad in fundamental position

Piece without a dominant seventh

Piece with diminished triad in second inversion

Piece ending with an inverted chord

(b) Figured Bass. Examples from seventeenth century studied and performed. Similar examples constructed.

Sixteenth through eighteenth weeks:

Further study of seventh chords. Dissonant tones and chords. Specific examples of each point covered to be brought in by students (as found in familiar repertoire). Listening to works played by instructor on piano, or on records, for recognition of harmonic sounds and connections in context.

Material used:

Schubert: Mass

Christmas carols

Haydn: Seven Last Words

Nineteenth through twenty-second weeks:

Further study of harmony as applied to simple harmonic forms, leading to first study of sonata form (sonata allegro).

Material used:

Veracini: B-Flat Sonata for Violin and Piano

K. P. E. Bach: F Minor Piano Sonata
Beethoven: Trio for Clarinet, Cello, and Piano,
    Opus 11
Mozart: F Minor Fantasie for Organ, K. 608

Twenty-third week:

Test:

(*a*) harmony:
1. short chorale
2. figured bass

(*b*) identification and recognition of style (records)
1. work by Lassus
2. sonata (violin and piano) of Mozart
3. work by Ravel
4. work by Bach
5. Stravinsky: Symphony of Psalms

Twenty-fourth week:

Writing assignment and discussion: variations on an original theme for trumpet or clarinet, with contrasting rhythm for wood-block.

Twenty-fifth week:

Beginning study of thematic relationship and relation between movements, in works of classical and romantic periods.

Material used:
Mozart: G Minor Symphony (No. 25)
Beethoven: Symphony No. 4
Schumann: Symphony No. 4

Twenty-sixth week:

Concentration on aural analysis:
Extensive study of performed works, without score
Extensive study of performed works, with score
Extensive study of works from score only (not performed)

Material used:
Haydn: "Farewell" Symphony

     Berlioz: Benvenuto Cellini Overture
     Piston: Flute Sonata

Final weeks:
    Concentration on improvisation, illustrating:
       sequences
       various harmonic rhythms
       melodies in various styles
       general dramatic shapes
       simple modulations

Instructor C:

The subject of phrase and phrasing was the underlying motif of the whole course. My general approach was a blend of the chronological, on different levels; that is, simultaneous study and analysis of two different periods, but preserving a sort of double order. Works of all periods and for all media were analyzed in class and given as listening assignments. Orchestral instruments were discussed and listened to in class. Study of interval, scale, mode, and melody was emphasized in first four weeks; harmony begun in fifth week, with study of melody continued. Study of form was approached by analysis started at very beginning of semester.

    Students were asked to purchase:
      Beethoven: Third Symphony
             Prometheus Overture
      Mozart: Piano Concerto, K. 595
            Magic Flute Overture
      Bach: Fourth Brandenburg Concerto
      Diller–Quaile: Fourth Solo Book
      Harris: *Singing Through the Ages*
Hindemith's *Traditional Harmony* and Piston's *Harmony* were used and recommended.

    After the first opening talk, explaining the objectives of L & M, I never lecture if I can avoid it. As soon as possible I try to make the classes into a "workshop." We had quite a bit of free-for-all discussion in class; plenty of digression, too, some providing the most interesting moments in the class. I placed a great deal of emphasis on written technical work: melodic writing and composition assignments, both free and "in-the-style-of." The most dramatic and exciting moment in the course was when a piano student, after a careful analysis, played a short piece by Corelli without notes and without ever having read through it previously at the keyboard. The rest of the class was fully aware of what had happened and saw the value of this approach to their own music study.

A complete outline of sessions in this class is appended.

First class session:

    Explanation of objectives of the course

    Discussion of subject of listening, based on excerpts from:

        Copland's *What to Listen for in Music*

        Schoenberg's article in November 1946 issue of *Modern Music*

    Material used by students:

        Beethoven's Eighth Symphony—used for melodic and rhythmic dictation, with students singing, clapping, and conducting

Second class session:

    Original melody written in class

    Chord tune—scale tune

    Discussion of the overtone series

    Played third movement of Brahms' Third Symphony; students made written comments on everything they could hear, with special emphasis on points of interest

Third class session:

    Began demonstration of instruments of the orchestra by student playing trombone and giving report about his instrument, showing the overtones, etc.

Read article by Thomson: "Modern Methods of Composition"

Played two movements of Prokofiev's Fifth Symphony; discussion

Assignments: Write melody for your instrument; play it; sing it; edit. Listen to two symphonic works; arrange as program, with program notes. Pianists substitute a concerto. Singers listen to two groups of songs. Write overtone series for G, E-flat, F.

Second and third weeks:

Continued demonstration of instruments by students:

> (*a*) the violin
> (*b*) the flute
> (using the various people I had in class)

Began study of the modes

Melodic intervals used in plain song. (Singing examples from *Singing Through the Ages*, Harris; each student had his own book.)

Demonstration of Gregorian Chant by choral group

Report on Gregorian Chant by student

Began study of Beethoven's Third Symphony, each student having his own score

Assignments:

> *Ecclesiastical Modes*, Grove
> *Plainsong Accompaniment*, J. F. Arnold
> *Sixteenth Century Counterpoint*, Merrill
> Listen to Gregorian Chant
> Listen to Beethoven Symphonies Nos. 7, 4, 6
> Listen to Mozart G-Minor Symphony
> Listen to Haydn Oxford Symphony

Fourth and fifth weeks:

Read introduction to *Singing Through the Ages*, Harris

Records used illustrating different meters, different rhythmic designs, e.g., Debussy's "Festivals," Tschaikowsky's Pathetic Symphony

Demonstration of clarinet and oboe

Singing of Gregorian Chant

Examples of modes used by different composers

Dictation of modal melody

Finished first and second movements of the Beethoven Third Symphony

Assignments:

> Listening to record where clarinet and oboe were featured; trombone and flute, also

> Listening to records of Gregorian Chant, the troubadours and Minnesinger

Sixth and seventh weeks:

> Sang examples of French and Italian chanson, trouvères, etc.

> Melody writing—inversion of melodic group—mirror writing

> Through early types of counterpoint—organum, descant, faux-bourdon

> Played Debussy's "Engulfed Cathedral" and Harris' "Third Symphony"

> Began writing two-part counterpoint, my intention being to give only a few assignments in this

> Discussion of sixteenth century melody

> Demonstration of bassoon

> Gave test No. 1: to write a Kyrie (single-line melody)

> Assignment: Examples of early polyphonic music

Eighth and ninth weeks:

> Discussion of test; correction of counterpoint

> Dictation of rounds; singing

> Analysis of melodies in song book

> Analysis of melody—Schubert Unfinished Symphony

> Demonstration of horn

> Demonstration of bass clarinet

> Beginning harmony:

>> Discussion of intervals and triads; joining triads through common tone

>> Melodic and rhythmic dictation

In assignments accompanying the study of Beethoven's Eroica, comparable forms were listened to
in other works, for example:
> first movement, Sonata Allegro
> second movement, Rondo
> third movement, Scherzo—Minuet and Trio
> fourth movement, Theme and Variation

The fugues encountered brought up the discussion of
other fugues, which were listened to, e.g., Beethoven's
Seventh and Ninth Symphonies

Assignments embraced melody writing; six melodies in
different meters, different modes, different phrase
lengths

Tenth and eleventh weeks:

Test on sonata form

Test on theme and variation form

Records played; student to write the facts—what he
heard

Primary triads in root position

Began study of Bach Chorales

Demonstration of trumpet and tuba

Study of non-harmonic tones

Began study of Brandenburg Concerto No. IV, with
scores

Played modern music, e.g., "Music for the Theatre"
(Copland), "American Festival Overture" (W. Schuman)

Listening assignments now include Bach, Handel, and
contemporaries

Twelfth and thirteenth weeks:

Adding new harmonic resources such as sixth chords
and secondary triads in root position

Discussion of triads, after playing of "Appalachian
Spring"

Singing of chorales and discovery of familiar harmonic
material

Also, examples brought to class from the music which students are studying on their instruments

Bach Chorales—used in dictation, but really too difficult at this point

Studied first and second movements of Brandenburg Concerto

Compared first movement form of Brandenburg Concerto with sonata form

Further study of non-chord tones

Fourteenth and fifteenth weeks:

Finish Brandenburg Concerto

Finish "Appalachian Spring"

Analysis of C Minor Fugue, Book I, Well-Tempered Clavichord

Current listening assignment includes Bach Cantata, Prelude and Fugue, Dance Suites, Handel Concerto Grosso, Bloch Concerto

Written harmony being done each week, in conjunction with the singing and analysis of chorales

Sixteenth and seventeenth weeks:

Dominant sevenths

Secondary dominant sevenths

Putting basses under selected folk-song melodies

Began study of Mozart's Piano Concerto in B-Flat Major, K. 595, students using their scores. Comparing first movement form with Brandenburg Concerto first movement.

Continuing with Bach Chorales

Listening to Stravinsky's "Symphony of Psalms"

Listening assignments now are concerned with Mozart operas (Così fan Tutte, Marriage of Figaro, Don Giovanni), as background for L & M Wednesday concerts

Eighteenth and nineteenth weeks:

Continuation of harmony

Continuation of Mozart concerto

Special attention in small groups given to weak students

Twentieth and twenty-first weeks:

Second inversions of triads

Inversions of dominant sevenths, with pertinent illustrations

Discussion of diminished seventh chords

Early and late string quartets of Beethoven contrasted

Early and late piano sonatas

Listening now includes chamber music—examples of sonatina form

Finish Mozart concerto

Twenty-second and twenty-third weeks:

Secondary seventh chords

Modulation

Simple alteration

Study of Schubert songs

Song beautifully performed by one of the singers in the class

Beginning the study of small pieces; students each have a copy of *Fourth Solo Book* (Diller and Quaile)

Assignment: To write a saraband on a bass of Corelli.

Twenty-fourth and twenty-fifth weeks:

Played pieces written by class

Studied Schumann songs

Detailed analysis, formal and harmonic, of pieces in *Fourth Solo Book*, for example:

Corelli: Gigues

Rameau: Rondeau

Schumann: Album Leaves

Listening now covers nineteenth century literature

Homework: analysis of Magic Flute Overture—scores used

Twenty-sixth and twenty-seventh weeks:

Brahms songs

Italian Symphony (Mendelssohn)

Analysis of pieces—continuation of work in *Fourth Solo Book*

Twenty-eighth, twenty-ninth, and thirtieth weeks:

Began review

Bird's-eye view of harmony on an original saraband; developing the original simple structure by adding new resources

Listening is continued through nineteenth century composers and including impressionistic music and early Schoenberg.

During the last classes, a good deal of contemporary music was played, including works by Hindemith, Bartók, Berg, Stravinsky, and others.

Final Assignment: Original pieces in binary and ternary forms.

Instructor D:

I. GENERAL METHODS USED IN CLASS:

1. *Lectures:*

I did a great deal of lecturing in this L & M class. Most of it was impromptu at any point where I felt clarification for general background was necessary before proceeding, when conclusions or summings up were needed at the end of class discussion, or in the wake of a tangent that was pursued as a result of a question by a student. I gave four "premeditated" lectures on the following subjects: an introductory lecture on the course at the beginning, citing general objectives and methods, and briefly the basic philosophy of our approach; a second was given on melodic writing with examples and pertinent terminology; the third was on the subject of "traditional harmony in perspective"; and the last preceded the general discussion in which student impressions of the course were aired.

2. *Checking assignments:*
   Important assignments I checked thoroughly—some in class with the class making comments. Other assignments I spot-checked, criticizing without grading.

3. *Analysis of selected works:*
   We analyzed works of Palestrina, Bach, Mozart, Beethoven, Brahms, and Debussy in detail, using recordings for the orchestral works and performing vocal music or chamber music in class. Beyond this, each student did at least four individual assignments in which he analyzed and performed for the class works ranging from sixteenth century music to a diversified group of contemporary works.

4. *Listening:*
   The listening fell into two categories: the first, rhythmic, melodic, and harmonic dictation in precise detail; the second, listening to works two or three times in performance and getting as much technical detail as possible from such relatively short acquaintance with them.

5. *Arguing and free-for-all discussions:*
   I tried to maintain an informal atmosphere with maximum latitude for self-expression on the part of the student at all times. There were free-for-all discussions, and strong opinions were expressed. Among first-year students I tried to foster open-mindedness, however, until they had achieved some sort of technical knowledge to provide fortification of an objective nature for their opinions.

6. *Lessons:*
   After we had made a survey of traditional harmony and harmonized both given and original melodies, we reviewed the whole subject, using Hindemith's *Traditional Harmony*, and taking up exercises from each chapter.

7. *Performances of and by students:*
In general, the performance of my first-year students was not good enough to be worth using extensively. All too often, the musical point to be made was obscured rather than served by inadequate performance.

II. MATERIALS USED:
1. *Materials used in class:*
   (*a*) Intensively:
   Folk-songs of all nationalities, Bach Chorales, Hindemith's *Traditional Harmony*, Mozart, Beethoven, and Brahms symphonies (one each), Palestrina Motet, and Debussy's "Preludes."
   (*b*) Casually:
   Casual use was made of varied works for all media and from all periods from the pre-Bach period to contemporaries. For example, representative madrigals, German and French songs and short piano pieces, Hindemith's "Mathis der Maler," Bartók's "Fourth String Quartet" and piano pieces, Copland's "El Salon Mexico," Harris' "Third Symphony," etc.
   (*c*) As references:
   Standard biographical material; Forsyth's *Orchestration*, Piston's *Harmony*, Goetschius' *Homophonic Forms of Musical Composition*, Alchin's *Applied Harmony*, Hindemith's *Elementary Musicianship*, and Grove's *Dictionary of Music and Musicians*.
   Scores and music: Scores and music for everything heard were used to the extent available.
   Records: Records were used for all but a few piano works, songs, and choral music.
2. *What materials were the students requested to purchase?*
Students purchased the following: Allen Irvine Mc-

Hose's *Teachers' Dictation Manual*, Hindemith's *Traditional Harmony*, Palestrina's "Adoramus Te," Mozart's "Symphony No. 39," Brahms' "Symphony No. 3," and one score purchased as an individual assignment.

III. EXERCISES AND ASSIGNMENTS GIVEN:

1. *How much emphasis on written technical work?*

All students did written analyses twice during the year, employing such technical knowledge as they had at that point. Two or three assignments a week were given while reviewing Hindemith's *Traditional Harmony*.

2. *How much "free" composition?*

Each student did twelve or fifteen "free" compositions. Those with creative gifts enjoyed and benefited from this kind of work, and all of them learned a great deal about form from writing.

3. *How much "in-the-style-of" composition?*

"In-the-style-of" composition has never seemed of value to me, so I did not use it.

4. *Other types of exercise, etc.*

We tried a few class creative projects, e.g., the entire chorale melody to be used for a "harmonization" assignment would be written by the class—"creating out loud," as it were, in the class; learning to sing entire harmonic structure of a given piece around any given part.

One can sum up these approaches in a general sense. All are designed to keep the student in active relation with the art of music while he is learning the fundamentals of musical techniques. All introduce the student to a variety of musical styles, forms, and idioms, many of them previously unfamiliar. All of them accomplish the examinable results (as a minimum) of the usual first-year harmony course, but in addition they provide a basis for placing this "harmony" in a useful perspective, in its relation to polyphony, form, or even history. In all these approaches also, "traditional harmony" has not been set up as a musical norm from which contemporary music must be considered an odd deviation or an "incorrect" one.

The use of actual music at all times involves one further point of the greatest importance in the L & M curriculum. It is not to be expected that a beginning student will be able to penetrate much below the surface of a given musical work. It is therefore quite usual for the L & M teacher to make recurrent or "progressive" use of certain works at various stages of the student's advancement. Thus, a student in his second year may go more deeply into techniques and problems of a work that he first heard, and examined, in his first year. He may find additional points of interest, new values. In his third year, he may meet the same work again. Each study will have a wider scope, more numerous bases for comparison, firmer grasp of historical and technical premises. The student will also have grasped an idea of re-examination and re-appraisal that should benefit him throughout his musical life and should help to make him both independent and patient in his musical thinking and should perhaps persuade him that no knowledge and no conclusions are necessarily final.

In the study of modes, for example, the student during the first year may:

1. sing examples of plain chant (*Liber Usualis* and other sources).

2. become acquainted, through lecture and example, with the theoretical and practical forms of the common ecclesiastical modes.

3. grasp the idea, through singing and listening, of a meter and prosody that are not dependent on harmony. (This will later be shown to be of vital importance to the understanding of contemporary music. Examples from contemporary music, particularly with respect to contemporary use of modes, may be introduced in the first year.)

4. write modal melodies, with and without bar-lines, and with and without text.

5. listen to representative examples (on records, or possibly in classroom performance) such as:

     (*a*) Gregorian Chant

     (*b*) Organum

     (*c*) Ars Nova

     (*d*) Flemish and Italian polyphony.

6. become acquainted with characteristic "vertical" sounds in modal music and learn to recognize characteristic cadences (Landino, Josquin).

This is perhaps a good deal for the first-year student, and it is not to be expected that the amount of absorption or retention will be extremely high. We do expect, and have found in practice, that the first-year student retains a foundation on which he can build and expand, so that constant reference to many of the above points or procedures becomes profitable and meaningful in an increasing measure. The gradual transformation of modes and the evolution of tonality can be explored in the second or third year, and again and again where necessary, as in the study of sixteenth and seventeenth century examples, and in relation to contrapuntal or harmonic practices that may absorb the student's attention at a given time.

HARMONY

The study of "harmony" is begun in the first year but is approached in many ways. An effort is made in all cases to suggest to the student that so-called "traditional" harmony is a practice but not a *criterion*. It is not invariably necessary that harmony be approached as a matter of four-part chorale style; some instructors have effectively used the simpler Schubert songs as an introduction to the subject. But if the Bach Chorales are taken as a focal point for the study of certain aspects of tonal harmony, they are not therefore to be taken as the standard of comparison for, let us say, the Psalms of Schütz, a chorale by Stravinsky, a "chordal" passage in Josquin. The L & M teacher, however he touches upon "harmony," is also careful not to isolate it; he will emphasize connection and point out that harmony is a function of motion, *of a certain kind*. He will introduce, even at an early stage, ideas of cadence, phrase, direction, structure.

The formation of chords must be learned by the student through ear, eye, and hand. He will find examples in music, as well as illustrations on the blackboard. He is expected to be able to identify and reproduce simple chords with facility. All students in L & M receive basic keyboard instruction (about which, more below) so that they can test and practice notes sounded simultaneously. At the same time, to avoid the curse of "piano thinking," the class will experiment with playing, thinking, and hearing chords on various instruments, or sung in various registers.

Nomenclatures of course require a certain amount of "rote" teaching. There are terms that must be defined and illustrated before a study of "harmony" can be undertaken: major, minor, interval, triad, resolution, cadence, scale, and others. It is important that all these be understood through the ear as well as through the eye. It is not expected, in normal cases, that these necessary preliminaries should occupy much time. What is important is that much other material, and many other references, may be introduced while a definition of terms is in progress. The overtone series and its relation to temperament and harmony may, for example, be illustrated by a trombone player in the class, who will, at the same time, acquaint the class with the range, timbre, and characteristics of the instrument. Other instruments may be utilized for similar purposes. It is, for example, often a rewarding experiment in learning intervals to allow a pianist to attempt to tune a violin; the pianist emerges, as a rule, with a new respect for the perfect fifth. The instructor can, and should, illuminate his approach to basic elements of music with as wide as possible a variety of musical reference and experience.

In some L & M classes, harmony textbooks are used; in others, their use is discouraged. This is a matter for the individual instructor to decide. He may require the purchase of a text (Piston, Hindemith, or any other), or he may merely cite or recommend the reading of one. "Traditional" harmony is, of course, to be covered thoroughly, although the *manner* in which this is done is left entirely to the judgment of the instructor. There are several basic points of agreement among the members of the L & M faculty with respect to the study of "traditional" harmony, and these must be emphasized strongly:

1. Harmony is not to be taught on the basis of exercises alone, nor on that of "analyzing" (that is, *naming*) chords or progressions.
2. "Traditional" harmony is derived from practice, not vice versa, and there are other practices, *both past and present*.
3. "Traditional" harmony is not a matter of naming or connecting chords. It is not of much use unless it is understood in terms of its structural or architectural use in classical forms, nor is it of much use unless its functions are heard and understood in terms of motion.

These ideas may be said to color the approach to harmony in the first years, as well as the later stages, of L & M. The concepts of harmony and tonality are viewed as constantly changing, as evolving toward and away from the classical "norm" of traditional usage.

Beyond the traditional "harmony book" and exercise method of familiarizing the student with the sound and manipulation of triads and chordal progressions, there are a number of approaches that may be utilized. A number of techniques have been found successful on the first-year level, and a few of these may be tabulated as follows:

1. through melody, with analysis of dissonant or nonchord tones;

2. through counterpoint, or the manipulation of changing vertical intervals in linear movement;

3. through composition of melodies over a limited vocabulary of two or three chords, as a preliminary to attempting the use of longer sequences of harmony;

4. through exercises or "compositions" using Alberti basses or other figures instead of block chords in chorale style (Schubert songs may be used as models);

5. through reduction of simple "classical" pieces to written-out harmonic progression in chorale style;

6. through expansion of simple chorales, by figuration and melodic embellishment, into little pieces for piano, voices, or instruments;

7. through constant comparative analysis of phrase and cadence in differing styles.

The over-all idea of the development of tonality through the exploration of harmonic relations, and the clarification of the force of harmony as motion to be directed and controlled, can be made clear only through extensive application of manifold examples. The instructor may, for example, illustrate specifically and technically the differences and relation among various works using the note E (Phrygian, major, minor) as a tone center. Examples might be chosen from such diverse composers as:

Josquin: Example in Davison-Apel, *Historical Anthology of Music*, Vol. I, No. 90 (HAM)
Scheidt: Görlitzer Tabulaturbuch
Handel: Trio Sonata in E

Mendelssohn: Violin Concerto
Schubert: Schöne Müllerin, Nos. 18 and 20
Purcell: New Air on a Ground Bass
Beethoven: Sonata, Opus 90
Bach: Chorale
Brahms: "O wüsst Ich doch . . ."
Fauré: Tenth Nocturne
Chopin: Nocturnes, Opus 62, No. 2; Opus 72.
Ravel: Forlane ("Tombeau de Couperin")

These will be examined for cadence, phrase, adherence to (or deviation from) mode or scale, progressions, nonharmonic tones, as well as in terms of medium and expressive content. It goes without saying that the first-year student may find this quite a bit to assimilate. But let us assume that the student is willing to make the necessary effort to immerse himself in music. On whatever level he has reached, he will retain the ideas of comparison, of change, of relatedness; he will find his "harmony lesson" immeasurably broadened and made manifest in the context of art. He will realize (the instructor will have repeatedly emphasized the point) that many technical complexities are still beyond him, but he will have the expectation of exploring them at a later stage, perhaps through a return to these same works. In addition, the class as a whole will have accomplished the following "extra" results:

1. Heard a stimulating variety of music, much of it probably unfamiliar;

2. Identified and placed all the composers in terms of "music history";

3. Examined carefully the use of the Phrygian mode in Josquin's "familiar" style, and noted the survival of the Phrygian mode in later examples;

4. Compared versions of a chorale by Scheidt and Bach, and used both for sight-singing exercises;

5. In connection with the Purcell, the class will have examined and discussed a simple ground bass, and become acquainted with its technique. A simple bass of this sort may also be used for melodic dictation.

6. Students in the class will have performed the Handel Sonata as an ensemble assignment.

7. Performed the songs and piano music in class if students of requisite ability were present;

8. Compared the piano and orchestral versions of the "Tombeau de Couperin," and discussed orchestration;

9. Finally, as an assignment, each student will have been required to find similar examples on his own, and to report on these.

The attention of the student will be directed to specific technical problems in all of the styles represented. Harmonization of Bach Chorales (the familiar pedagogic technique) may be done concurrently with "free" harmonizations of simple melodies in the style, for example, of Mendelssohn's "Songs without Words." Other types, involving rudimentary or advanced ideas of tonality, may be attempted as the student's capabilities develop and as the instructor finds them useful. Figured bass, as a traditional usage, may be explored not only on the basis of "chorale style" but as employed in a Handel Concerto Grosso, a Corelli Trio Sonata, or a Bach Sonata for flute, violin, or cello. Realization of continuo parts (figured) at the keyboard or on paper, with examples taken from actual works of seventeenth and eighteenth century composers, is often used as a part of L & M teaching technique in this area. Such application of figured bass study leads naturally to the discussion of questions of style, and these may be suggested even in the early stages of study. Various "realized" editions may be compared for accuracy, appropriateness, and other qualities. Needless to say, such questions may be explored again and again as the student's knowledge widens.

It should be clear that all of the aspects of the study of harmony suggested above provide material for further and later study on a vastly expanded, and constantly expanding, scale. Questions of melody or of form and analysis lend themselves to similar treatment. The effort can be constantly renewed and attention frequently redrawn to problems first encountered at an early stage of L & M. In this way also, the student comes to realize that the possibility of learning about music, far from being a matter of completion of a curriculum, may well be limitless.

COUNTERPOINT

The study of counterpoint can be pursued concurrently with that of harmony and may begin at a very early stage. Here again, the imagination and judgment of the L & M instructor must determine how best to suit the needs of his students. In any case, the relation of "species" or academic counterpoint to L & M study follows the same lines as that of traditional harmony. In general, a survey of idioms will precede detailed study of any period or style, so that the student will be somewhat oriented as to the importance and relation of sixteenth century, eighteenth century, or other pedagogic "norms" of contrapuntal technique. It will certainly be pointed out by the instructor that there are contrapuntal techniques and usages other than those of the sixteenth or eighteenth centuries and that all must be considered in the full context of the music of their times. A contrapuntal survey on a beginning level, concentrating on counterpoint in two parts, may include such examples as the following:

Organa (Source: HAM or Gleason)
Forms of Ars Antiqua and Ars Nova (Source: HAM or Gleason)
Josquin: Pleni Sunt Coeli (Dessoff Choir Series)
Galilei: Contrappunti a due parti (Smith College)
Lassus: Two-part Motets (Dessoff Choir Series)
Handel, Purcell, and Couperin: Keyboard pieces
Bach: Two-Part Inventions; French Suites
Examples of two-part counterpoint in Mozart and Beethoven
Examples in Hindemith, Bartók (Mikrokosmos), Milhaud, Stravinsky, Krenek, Riegger, Webern

As with the examples cited above in connection with "harmony," these contrapuntal examples will all be sung or played in class by the students. They will be analyzed in terms of note-against-note relations, rhythmic opposition, juxtaposition of phrase, and quality of line. Many factors other than contrapuntal techniques will come to the attention of the class and will be discussed. These will include the subjects of phrase, cadence, timbre, among others. The nature and evolution of the simpler contrapuntal forms will be examined, with perhaps additional examples. Relationships of compositional techniques to performance are sure to occupy considerable attention. This may be illustrated by a classroom example arising from discussion and analysis of the first Two-Part Invention of Bach. Students bring to class their own copies; it is usually found that a number of editions will be brought in and that students performing from these will vary considerably in matters of tempo and phrasing. Comparison of editions brings to light the fact that tempo markings alone (Czerny, Mason, Griepenkerl, et al.) vary from 76 to 120 for the quarter note! The students are compelled to consider, in an analytical way *specifically directed at performance*, the relation of harmony (harmonic rhythm) to tempo, the relation of tempo to form, and a multitude of other problems affecting understanding and interpretation in the most cogent way. It is in such terms that "analysis" of an Invention may provide a real foundation for the student, beyond the acquisition of facility in writing imitative exercises in eighteenth century counterpoint.

Manners of "teaching" counterpoint in L & M classes are varied. Here again, textbooks may be used or not, as the instructor decides, though it may be said that in general textbooks are not recommended to any extent. At a

certain stage, it is often found to be of pedagogic utility
to suggest that the student compare, as a home-study assignment, a number of "authoritative" counterpoint texts,
forming his own conclusions as to their relative value.
The nature of "rules," and their relation to musical practices, may be further clarified as a result of such an assignment. L & M instructors approach the question of species
counterpoint in varying ways. All touch upon it in terms
of its derivation, its historical justification, its possible
value as a teaching tool. It may be suggested that the student read Fux, or the introductory chapters of Jeppesen's
Counterpoint, or Piston, or Volume II of Hindemith's
Craft of Musical Composition. The instructor may himself synthesize, or help the student formulate, a set of
"rules" taken from Kitson, Koechlin, Richardson, Prout,
Lavignac, and others; but he will always attempt to make
clear that only a schematization of actual practice is
thereby suggested and that the important study always
remains the music itself from which any formulation may
derive. Some instructors require students to keep notebooks of "do's and don't's" observed in the musical examples studied and to formulate therefrom a handbook of
practical contrapuntal rules as applied to various styles.
In some classes, the usual exercises in species counterpoint
are given considerable attention, while in others this aspect of study is treated only in passing. In some classes,
the various "species" are treated in sixteenth, seventeenth,
eighteenth, nineteenth, and twentieth century styles, the
students being required to discover examples of characteristic patterns in the composers of all these periods.

REPORTS BY INSTRUCTORS—SECOND YEAR OF COURSE

Two examples of the manner of approach to contrapuntal studies in an L & M curriculum of the second-year level may be cited. These examples are taken from annual reports by the instructors.

Instructor A:

GENERAL METHOD USED IN CLASS:

The first week was spent in preparing students for the course as a whole, in giving a general picture of musical materials and the various techniques which were prevalent in their particular place in history. This was done in a chronological manner, emphasizing the evolutionary process of music. This was followed by a week of stressing, in a purely abstract way, the materials of the periods of music, from Gregorian Chant to the twentieth century—with clear musical examples. Trying to make the students see the musical picture as a whole immediately was meant to do two things:

1. to point out the vast amount of music that had been written before Bach
2. to make their minds flexible enough to be able to grasp the important periods of music from a reasonable perspective.

Occasionally during these early lectures, references to contemporary composers who were influenced by early composers or techniques were made. Experiments such as attempts at the quarter-tone scale during the Baroque era (by Vincentino) were also mentioned. This was done deliberately in the sense of "shock treatment," to arouse their musical curiosity enough to realize that the era of early music is not a dead one, but is regarded as very much alive by various contemporary composers.

Next, the periods of music were taken chronologically and in detail, starting with Gregorian Chant and followed by the discovery of polyphony, born of the attempt to sing the same melody simultaneously at a different pitch. The three styles of organum were studied (parallel, oblique, contrary), followed by the music of the Notre Dame school (Ars Antiqua), showing the two basic methods of writing (Leonin and Perotin). This was followed by the Ars Nova of the fourteenth century (Landini and Machaut in particular), the Burgundian and Netherlands schools (Dufay, Obrecht, Ockeghem, and Josquin in particular), and finally the sixteenth century Lassus and Palestrina, which served as a kind of middle point of polyphony. This was followed by the English and Italian madrigalists (Byrd, Wilbye, Marenzio, Gesualdo, Monteverdi), Purcell, Bach, Haydn, Mozart, and fragmentary representations from this period to the contemporary.

Each period was initiated by the singing of the music by the class as a whole, usually followed by repetition by a small group, followed again by singing of the whole group. We then analyzed the composition in class, always emphasizing intervals (vertical and horizontal), rhythm, individual melodic lines, and finally the structure of the piece as a whole. The cadences were analyzed as a unit, and also techniques which are representative of the period. After each significant piece was examined thoroughly and discussed, the students were required to use these principles in a composition of their own.

Being something new, the modal system was emphasized. Periodically, transposed modes were played at the keyboard and the students asked to recognize the mode. This was done with the intention of keeping the student constantly aware of modal sound as opposed to the diatonic system. Music which resulted from the simultaneous use of two or more parts, emphasizing melodic line, was contrasted to music which used a conscious chordal progression. During the change of the modal system to the diatonic system, the students were given factors of the latter's evolution. Before beginning and treating this somewhat changed musical language, the instructor gave the student abstract explanations (such as, the common triad constituted the nucleus of all other chord formations; every chord and chord progression and every key of modulatory scheme stood in clearly defined relation to a center, and, through it, to another). Comparisons were made to contemporary composers (such as, the intervallic sounds and cadences of the earlier periods with Hindemith, and the Viennese classic composers with later Stravinsky, and the partial key signatures with the polyharmonic key signatures of the 1920's).

Instructor B:

Points of primary emphasis in early meetings were:

(*a*) training of conscious hearing
(*b*) training toward understanding "expressive quality" or intellectual purpose of music of all periods
(*c*) attempt at developing ability to think about the bases of music and becoming literate about such fundamentals

Discussions in successive meetings centered on:

1. What is music?
2. What is melody?
3. Does music have a reason for being, and from what needs of humanity do the reasons stem?
4. What is relation of performer to the music community as a whole?

Readings in selected estheticians for purposes of centralizing thinking about art problems.

(*d*) Discussions on difficulties of music as a profession, and the need for a genuine interest in music itself.

Beginning technical studies were based on an attempt to direct experience derived from knowledge of simple triad structures into terms of music and included weekly short compositions with continued emphasis toward thinking in terms of line rather than "block" chords. Success of this venture could not be measured in terms of gain in technical facility, but in the beginnings of the realization that technical gains could come only from direct consideration of the problems of music values. Full realization of this among the better students came later. Personal criticism was afforded each student by dismissing body of class and retaining only a few for private conference.

Listening methods during this period were premised on need for general background as well as a correlation with harmonic studies: chromatic harmonies, modulations, key relationships and the reasons for them, sound masses without tonal center and purposes, harmonic direction over extended time length, differences between "static" and "movement" harmonies, effect of individual line on all of these. Materials used included Mozart-Haydn string quartets, Bach-Brahms choral music sung in class and performed on records.

After carrying out such studies as far as the students' capacities would allow, an abrupt change was felt necessary. Direction was changed toward simple melodic structure: analysis and construction of second "germ" which would effect a counterpoint with the first, and finally extension of second to full counterpoint. Procedure was repeated over two-week period, and another abrupt change was made with an assignment of composition of a complete movement of a string quartet for all students but string players; a woodwind quartet for string players. No definite time limit placed on students for completion of this project. "Classic period" example afforded if desired.

Listening now directed toward pattern studies of classic string quartets, explanations and demonstrations of string and woodwind instruments, problems of kind of material used for specific instruments and combinations (i.e., music material), instrumental sonorities and effects, harmonic and contrapuntal effects used as compositional devices. Examples of early period contrapuntal study.

Quartets duly received, criticized, revised, rechecked, parts extracted, performed in class. Time for class criticism limited because of great time expense. General reaction quite favorable; students learned something about expressive needs and control; many of the compositions had considerable intrinsic interest; a great deal of harmonic experimentation was undertaken with only rare examples of any success. Most stimulating procedure thus far in the course. In fact, from that time on, little or no force mechanism was needed on my part to keep the classes moving. I was, then (as I had expected to be from the beginning), merely a director of traffic.

Intensive work begun in contrapuntal training, using as principal mechanics the two-part canon. All canons scored for instruments present in class; all performed. Particular emphasis placed on strength of line, weaknesses being very obvious in canonic performance. Class participation in criticism of student compositions became much more valid and worth while in this procedure. Continued with attempts at more complicated canons than at the octave or unison. Followed with analysis of series of Bach Inventions, after which students wrote Inventions of their own, using procedural method of again constructing "germs" or "motives," criticism, and then full evolution of ideas. Emphasis on inventiveness. Concentration on chromaticism and patternization, first in Bach works and then in students' works. Again performed in class. Procedure culminated with an examination on students' ability to analyze a Bach Invention on their own.

Listening procedures becoming more exacting as to technical resources, style, period, etc. Particular emphasis placed on early periods of music where compositional resources are yet simple enough for students' ability to hear exactly and economically. Class singing again re-emphasized (never having been completely omitted), the analysis and discussion of materials of contrapuntal usage being the principal subject material.

Following this, a further development of canonic study was made for a two-week period, mainly for purposes of attaining concentration again after recess, and from that point to end of semester a relatively complete review was undertaken.

By the middle of the second year, on the average, the student will have a working acquaintance at least with "traditional" and other techniques of harmony; will have studied and written examples of two-part counterpoint in various styles, including, of course, invertible counterpoint; and will have made some progress toward the definition and understanding of historical and stylistic phenomena. He will have surveyed, through study and *participation in performance*, the history of Western music, including that of the present day as well as of the remoter past. "Early" music and "modern" music will, it is hoped, have assumed some reality for him, as well as some previously unsuspected values. In these terms, the music of "common practice" should itself appear in a new light.

The student should be, by this time, prepared to undertake a related (harmony-counterpoint-form-history) study such as the following. This series of classes, covering about two months, is also taken from an instructor's report and may be taken as a specific example in practice of L & M teaching in the second year.

Instructor C:

The "subject" of the series of classes is the chorale melody, "Allein Gott in der Höh sei Ehr." Versions of the melody, from its earliest sources to its form in Bach, are sung, studied, and compared; the implications in terms of modal polyphony and tonal harmony are considered. From this point, the following studies and assignments are undertaken.

Each student in class selects or is assigned a different chorale melody to be used in assignments below.

STUDY 1. Praetorius: "Allein Gott . . ." treated in two-part vocal counterpoint (choral motet).

Assignment: Class writes two-part choral motet in this style, using given chorale melody.

STUDY 2. J. S. Bach: Two-part keyboard setting (Bicinium) of "Allein Gott . . ." (Cantus firmus counterpoint).

Assignment: Class writes running sixteenth-note counterpoint above or below given chorale melody.

STUDY 3. J. S. Bach: Chorale harmonizations (four-part) of same melody (Nos. 125, 249, 313, 326 in Breitkopf edition).

Assignment: Class does four-part chorale harmonization; compares, rewrites.

STUDY 4. Schütz: Four-part Psalm setting (1628) of melody similar to "Allein Gott. . . ."

Compare with number three.

STUDY 5. Scheidt: Four-part harmonization of "Allein Gott . . ." in Görlitzer Tabulaturbuch (1650).

STUDY 6. Scheidt: Bicinium on Chorale, from Tabulatura Nova.

Compare with number two above.

STUDY 7. Pachelbel: Choral Prelude on "Allein Gott. . . ."

Assignment: Class attempts simple chorale prelude similar to Pachelbel.

STUDY 8. Elaborate harmonic presentation of melody by Bach (Arnstadt Chorales; Bach Gesellschaft XXXIX, 44).

Assignment: Class takes simple four-part chorale, elaborates through introduction of harmonies further removed from tonal center, plus secondary sevenths, and "altered" chords.

STUDY 9. J. S. Bach: Short Chorale Prelude on "Allein Gott. . . ."

Compare with chorale preludes on same or similar melody by Buxtehude, Böhm, J. G. Walther.

STUDY 10. Pachelbel: Partita on a chorale melody.

STUDY 11. J. S. Bach: Chorale Partita (any, or several).

Assignment: Class attempts composition of similar chorale prelude or partita.

STUDY 12. Brahms: Chorale Prelude.

STUDY 13. J. S. Bach: Fughetta on "Allein Gott . . ." (Clavier-Übung, III).

Assignment: Class attempts composition of fughetta.

STUDY 14. J. S. Bach: Chorale Cantata No. 4 (Variations) "Christ Lag in Todesbanden."

Assignment: Students purchase score (Broude) for study and "analysis."

A series of classes such as the above produces a number of results beyond the obvious ones of familiarizing the student with specific techniques of harmony and counterpoint. The relation of harmony and bar-line, the evolution of tonality, certain historical perspectives are all illustrated. In addition, these musical examples all provide material for ear-training (dictation) and for performance. Non-pianists can be encouraged to play the simpler chorales and bicinia at the keyboard. Other Bach Chorales, in the form of melody and figured bass, may be used as illustrations, and by having the class fill in alto and tenor voices at sight, *by singing*.

A great deal of additional material will be touched upon during the series of classes outlined. Some of this will be put aside for detailed study in later classes; some will be used for side-by-side study and analysis. This material, all obviously related in terms of harmony-counterpoint-form, may include such examples as:

Chorales in:
    Chopin (Nocturnes)
    Schumann (Album for the Young)
    Wagner (Meistersinger)
    Bartók (Third Piano Concerto)
    Stravinsky (Histoire du Soldat)
    Cowell (Woodwind Quintet)
Note-against-note harmonization in "familiar" styles of:
    Josquin (HAM, Vol. I, No. 90)
    Palestrina (Stabat Mater)
Partitas by Frescobaldi (*Folia*), leading to *Folia* as treated by A. Scarlatti, Corelli, Vivaldi. This will lead to consideration of ground basses, chaconnes, passacaglias, harmonic variation forms, and techniques of various periods.

It is this type of *extension of relation* that we feel to be one of the important possibilities in L & M instruction. Only time and the ingenuity of the instructor set limitations on the classes, but these limitations can be posed as existing only in order for the student to go beyond them. The student will have time, not only in later classes, but *also after he leaves school,* for all the music he can absorb. It is this desire to absorb that we wish to encourage. If the instructor has shown how vast and rewarding the field of music is, how fascinating its problems, if he has indicated one or more avenues of exploration, he will have accomplished much.

One further point should be emphasized: in all the examples given above, the choice of music, as well as method, is variable. The instructor will constantly find new and fresh examples and will encourage the student to do the same. In this way, teaching, as well as studying, avoids the routine of repetition, and the useful life of the teacher is perhaps prolonged. This liberty to exercise the imagination is one of the most vital factors in the continuing enthusiasm of the L & M faculty.

KEYBOARD STUDIES

Keyboard studies are considered of particular importance during the first years and are given varying amounts of emphasis in later stages. *For students majoring in piano,* special classes are required. These classes, under a specialist in this field, cover techniques of sight-reading, figured bass, open-score reading, "keyboard harmony," and improvisation, and afford the piano student opportunity for the development of skill in these elements beyond the scope of the L & M class proper. The keyboard study classes are designed to supplement the work of both the major teacher and the L & M teacher. Administratively, all grades given by the teacher of keyboard studies are passed on to the L & M teacher, who notes them in the student's file and takes account of them in formulating the student's final grade for the semester.

KEYBOARD HARMONY STUDY (PIANISTS), 1952–1953

Prerequisites for the study are familiarity by mind and ear with major and minor scales, intervals, and triads; also, familiarity with general musical terms, e.g., mode, key, time signature, rhythm.

The aim of the course is to make intelligent readers of music, by using the piano for the following keyboard skills:

- (*a*) chord connection
- (*b*) figured bass
- (*c*) harmonization of melody
- (*d*) modulation
- (*e*) transposition
- (*f*) reading at sight
- (*g*) improvisation

The practical use of the above is to develop the student's ability

1. to grasp the melodic, the rhythmic, the harmonic, and the structural components of a composition
2. to memorize with assurance and rapidity
3. to accompany with understanding and resourcefulness
4. to cope with music other than piano literature
5. to meet creative needs as the dancer's accompanist

For students majoring *in other fields than piano*, keyboard studies take the form of class instruction by the

L & M teacher or assistants. The procedures governing this phase of study were outlined in a memorandum of the L & M Planning Committee as follows:

The following is offered as a suggestion only. It is expected that each instructor in L & M will wish to vary procedures according to the needs of his students and the work planned in L & M classes. In any case, it is recommended by the L & M Planning Committee * that the work in Keyboard Studies be divided between the instructor himself and the Fellows assigned to him, and that in no case should a Fellow or Fellows be given complete responsibility for this aspect of the work.

For each section of L & M, extra teaching hours and rooms will be made available so that suitable divisions of students may be made to facilitate the pursuit of keyboard work.

The basic idea in including Keyboard Studies with L & M is to aid in conveying materials of music through the use of the keyboard instrument.

It is suggested that, as a preliminary, students be divided into the following categories:

    (*a*) Non-pianists
    (*b*) Students who are not quite beginners at the keyboard
    (*c*) Students of moderate ability
    (*d*) Students who may be considered relatively competent in keyboard work

For non-pianists, the instruction should include elementary piano technique, simple sight-reading, and transposition. In addition, students in the second category should be expected to learn and prepare a few simple piano pieces. Students in the third and fourth categories might be given work under the following headings:

    1. Score reading at keyboard

* See Appendix 1.

2. Realization of figured bass at keyboard
3. Advanced sight-reading
4. Exercises in transposing
5. Improvisation

In addition, it will be expected that the relatively advanced keyboard students will learn a number of ensemble works for performance in class. The amount of concentration on any aspect of keyboard study will be determined by the individual instructor.

So far as arrangement of hours is concerned, it should be pointed out that students who are on approximately the same level may be handled in small groups if that is convenient. They may be given one hour per week, one-half hour twice a week, or two hours every other week, or time in any other apportionment that seems best. On the other hand, students may be met individually on a flexible schedule if that appears best to meet the needs. It is not necessary that each student be met each week, although approximately the same amount of time should be given to each student in class. The discretion of the instructor in this respect is absolute. It is to be expected that after the beginning of the semester problems will arise which should be discussed by the entire faculty. The Planning Committee will welcome all suggestions, comments, or criticisms and will endeavor to assist in working out details at all times.

The emphasis in all cases is on the requirement that the work pursued at the keyboard be related in a musical way to the work being done in the L & M class.

EAR-TRAINING AND SIGHT-SINGING

Special classes in ear-training and sight-singing, including elements of solfège, are also given in connection with L & M. Although these are designed primarily for majors in voice, they are open to any students specifically assigned by the L & M instructor. These classes also are conducted by a specialist, whose notes on the subject will be of interest:

These classes are held specially for singers, but other students are welcome to attend. Each group has about twenty students, and those with special difficulties are seen individually during the year in order to plan extra practice and to work out their problems.

Since sight-singing seems to be the problem-child of American musical education, subject to discussion about the innumerable systems invented to "put it over," much thought has been given to the planning of these classes. The first step is to make the students themselves find where their weaknesses lie in sight-singing. The quickest way for them to find out is to give the group a Morley three-part Canzonet to try out. It is sad to see the large variety of poor sight-reading.

The classes are organized to remedy this in the simplest direct way: no theory, no method, but plenty of drill, not in a set routine, but with variety to make the lesson alive and interesting musically.

The most urgent need being the mastering of intervals, oral practice is first given, starting with major and minor seconds sung upward and downward, working gradually up to sevenths. Exercises are made up on the spur of the moment, using a code on the blackboard to tell the students what intervals to sing and whether up or down. By pointing to these directions, one can "compose" original and free melodic lines as chromatic as one pleases, the students following directions and singing along completely unaided by harmonic background. This keeps interest very much alive, since they never know what they will sing.

For homework, material is written out: pages of exercises in intervals arranged in combinations of all possibilities. Naturally, too much of this can be bad and make students so interval-conscious that a melodic line is forgotten and only sensed as a series of skips. So, very obvious melodies having definite harmonic meaning are written, with the purpose of making students understand a phrase at once and of reading in advance to grasp the musical meaning. These are rewritten with variations, using chromatic notes and skips, yet keeping the tonal sense. In this way, we blend the interval-consciousness with the feel of a melodic line. New material is made up constantly.

Solfège books are invaluable for drill, to bring about confidence and stamina. After the complicated work in intervals, the Dannhauser Solfège Book No. 1 seems almost too obvious; but being asked to beat time as they sing, many students become aware of a new problem in the study of rhythmic coordination and get to sense beats rather than count them.

Since many students have been "contaminated" by the very limited "movable *do*" system used in public schools and cannot cope with modulations, syllables are not used. The ones who use the syllables in the "fixed *do*" system always do better than the others. But as long as the right sounds are produced, they can sing *la* or what they wish.

Solfège exercises are often broken up, each student singing two measures at a time. This forces them to follow, watch for their entrances, and develop a sense of timing. The piano is used to accompany solfège exercises, but never playing the given melody; the accompaniment is either above or below and often spiced with a musical sense of humor to take the dull edge off the not too exciting tunes.

To complement solfège books and enrich the class musically, fragments taken from all sorts of early and modern works are sung, especially those which contain difficulties of rhythm and intonation. In due time, a large amount of material will be collected.

To end the class, choral music is read, from early polyphonic works, parts of Bach Cantatas, modern arrangements of folk songs, etc. The piano is used only to fill in when the proportion of voices is weak. The plan is to have the students leave with a sense of musical well-being after concentrated drilling. Though perhaps too much may seem to be done in one hour of class, it is completely feasible if all is well planned in advance. Sometimes, one does more intervals, or more rhythm work, but it is good to end the class with music.

REPORTS OF INSTRUCTORS—PERFORMANCES IN CLASSES

It has already been pointed out that a considerable amount of music is performed and heard in L & M classes and group meetings. It is true, of course, that there are some practical limitations governing live performance in class: difficulty of works in terms of time needed for preparation, inadequate "instrumentation" in a given class, or specialized problems of style in performance. Reports of two instructors, however, will show that much can be accomplished.

Instructor A:

I should like to comment on the L & M class "general organization" meetings . . . which seem to me one of the most valuable features of the L & M program at the present time.

During 1952–1953, I met my entire group of L & M students once every week for an hour and a half. This period turned out to be a combination class-discussion forum and class concert hall. Subjects too specialized or "off-beat" to lie within the ordinary range of study could be presented here, deriving a particularly rich variety of reactions, comments, and contributions in discussion and analysis from the presence of first-, second-, third-, and fourth-year student pianists, singers, wind players, string players, and percussionists of different capacities and experience, participating on an equal footing. Some of the projects were suggested and prepared by the students themselves. One advanced student, not a conducting major, asked permission to present the Brahms Alto Rhapsody, and did so, using the entire class as orchestra and chorus. The result, achieved with a minimum of teacher guidance, and with only two hours' time available, was a performance good enough to illuminate our analysis of the work in a quite exciting way. Another project was the performance in succession of the Vivaldi concerto for four violins and string orchestra, followed by the Bach concerto for four pianos and strings, with sections repeated for more detailed comparison. My 1952–1953 class had no conducting majors, but at least eight of the advanced students found opportunities to conduct at the general meetings. These students were encouraged to lead and stimulate the class discussion and analysis as part of their assignments.

Instrumentalists, singers, or ensemble groups who had some important or particularly interesting work in process of study were encouraged to use the general meeting as a trial concert hall, which provided a continuing backlog of live performances on which to draw, as well as good preliminary experience for the performers without quite the tension of a formal school concert.

Whenever outstanding work, in written or composed assignments, was done in our other classes, whether elementary or advanced, we re-played and discussed these pieces at the general meetings. This was particularly useful in giving the beginning students an idea of what their more advanced colleagues were doing, and vice versa.

For the preparation of more difficult contemporary works (Stravinsky, Milhaud, and others), a chamber orchestra group was set up, and rehearsal time allotted. Although we were limited to players and singers who were quite unevenly matched as to ability and experience, the results were sufficiently good for some of these works, originally played and studied at our Tuesday meetings, to be repeated later at formal school concerts.

Besides a large number of works from the more familiar periods, our meetings also surveyed off-the-beaten-track aspects of the repertoire, such as music of Gesualdo, Ives, Harry Partch (composer of American *sprech-stimme* music, using a 43-tone scale with newly-devised instruments), and also African, Indian, and Balinese "ethnic" music, as well as "shape-note" American music and some samples of medieval music, with discussions of systems of notation.

My impression is that the new students, in particular, derived much from this experience of ranging freely over a vast musical territory. Not everyone enjoyed or approved of each kind of music studied, but I felt that the L & M concept of music as an immense, many-sided phenomenon began to be understood and even taken quite for granted as the year progressed.

The above report may be taken as representative. Instructor B's report consists solely of the list of specific works performed by students in his class at the weekly general meetings during 1952–1953:

Instructor B:

October 21: Purcell: Suite from "The Double Dealer" (strings, student conductor)

October 28: Vivaldi: Sonata in G Minor, for Flute and Continuo (harpsichord and 'cello)

Contemporary pieces for unaccompanied flute

November 4: Orlando Gibbons: Three-part Fantasias (strings)

Handel: Trio Sonata, E Major, Opus 2

November 11: Telemann: Arias and Duets (voice, strings, keyboard)

Schumann: *Dichterliebe*

November 18: Schubert: Four Songs from *Die Winterreise*

Muffat: Suite from "Florilegium Musicum" (strings, student conductor)

November 25: Spohr: Quintet for Piano and Winds, Opus 52

Wanhal: Sonata for Clarinet and Piano

December 2: Vivaldi: Trio Sonata, Opus 1, No. 1

J. C. Bach: String Trio, Opus 4, No. 2

December 9: Two-, three- and four-part music for vocal ensembles, by Landino, Josquin, Lassus, Sermisy, de la Rue (student conductor)

December 16: Corelli: "Christmas" Concerto (strings, student conductor)

Chopin: Ballade, F Minor

January 6: Mozart: Concerto in A Major, for Piano and Orchestra, K. 488 (student soloist and conductor)

January 13: Prokofiev: Piano Sonata No. 3

Persichetti: "The Hollow Men" for Trumpet and Strings (student soloist and conductor)

January 20: Debussy: *Proses Lyriques*

Schumann: Andante and Variations (two-piano version)

January 27: Orchestrations by advanced students, performed by members of class

February 3: Handel: Arias from oratorios

Brahms: Late piano pieces

February 10: Orchestrations by advanced students

February 17: Beethoven: Sonata in A Major for 'Cello and Piano, Opus 69

February 24: Honegger: Sonatina for Clarinet and Piano

De Menasce: Sonata No. 1 for Violin and Piano

March 3: Mozart: Concerto in G Major, for Piano and Orchestra, K. 453 (student soloist and conductor)

March 10:	Mozart: Variations (Piano) on March from *Mariage des Samnites*
	Debussy: *Danses* for Harp and Strings (student soloist and conductor)
March 17:	Schoenberg: Piano Pieces, Opus 19
	The same, scored for chamber orchestra by a third-year student
March 24:	Fauré: Sonata No. 1 for Violin and Piano
	Stravinsky: Sonata for Two Pianos
March 31:	Wagenaar: Concertino for Eight Instruments (student conductor)
April 14:	Franck: Sonata for Violin and Piano
April 21:	Galliard: Sonata for Bassoon and Piano
	Haydn: Sonata in C Major for Piano (B & H No. 48)
April 28:	Mozart: Concerto in G Major for Violin and Orchestra, K. 216 (student soloist and conductor)
May 5:	Hindemith: Sonata in E Major for Violin and Piano
May 12:	Chopin: Sonata in B Minor for Piano, Opus 58

L & M CONCERTS

To supplement the work in L & M classes, and to provide a steady fare of good performances of works of varied musical interest, a series of "L & M Concerts" was instituted in 1950 and has been continued ever since. These concerts, taking place each Wednesday noon, and lasting one hour, are given under the auspices of the L & M faculty, and attendance is required for all students registered in L & M courses. These concerts are not open to the public, but all students and members of the faculty are invited.

Suggestions for works to be performed at these concerts come not only from the L & M faculty, but also from the major and chamber music faculties. The preparation of the performance is usually undertaken by a major teacher or a member of the chamber music faculty, although occasionally performances prepared in L & M classes (as noted by Instructor "A," above) are of a sufficiently high standard to merit inclusion on a Wednesday program. The quality of the performance is the responsibility of the teacher in whose class it is prepared; the L & M concert committee, and the Concert Department of the School, do not attempt to select or "screen" performers.

The L & M committee delegated to work out the Wednesday programs often suggests lists of works to other faculties, for possible preparation and performance. The Wednesday concerts are not designed to replace or supplement student recitals or public concerts given at the School, although they do of course provide opportunities for gifted students to appear before fellow students and faculty members. The primary concern of the L & M faculty is that the Wednesday concerts should serve as an adjunct to the L & M curriculum itself, and that the music performed should represent a widely catholic selection. Although standard repertoire is not neglected, a primary objective of the concerts is the extension of knowledge of repertoire in all categories. It is felt that the musical education of all students will best be served by a widely representative selection of music of all types and periods.

The usefulness of the concerts is manifold. Not only

is much music, familiar and unfamiliar, heard by the students in live performances, but often works studied beforehand are placed in a new perspective—that of actual concert performance. In many L & M classes, students are required to keep notebooks of comment, analysis, or criticism of all works performed at the Wednesday concerts. Here again, the first-year or second-year student is not expected, as a rule, to make profound observations, but he *is* expected to form the habit of listening to music with his whole mind, to develop and enlarge his consciousness in hearing and apprehending. More, of course, is to be expected of advanced students; here occasionally, one finds a very high level of appreciative and critical perception.

Undoubtedly the best comment on these concerts is afforded by the programs themselves. The Wednesday concert programs of one year (1950–1951) are therefore given in their entirety (names of performers deleted) in Appendix 3-A. Following these programs, as Appendix 3-B, will be found the programs of the public concerts (Friday evening series) given at the School during the same year. Although Juilliard students are not required to attend the Friday evening concerts, they are encouraged to do so, and music performed on these programs often is used for discussion purposes in L & M classes. With the two formal series of concerts, plus the great number of student recitals under the auspices of various individual major teachers, the student is afforded extensive opportunities for listening to live performances within the school and at no expense to himself. He is expected to supplement this already considerable quantity and variety of listening experience by taking advantage of the active concert life of New York. Student tickets at reduced rates, and in many cases free tickets, are distributed by the Juilliard Concert Office for most of the musical attractions offered "downtown." The student is expected to take advantage of all of these opportunities; it is by listening to music all the time, and at the highest level of consciousness, that we expect him, in the long run, to become a cultivated listener as well as a sensitive performer.

PART IV

Special Studies in the Third and Fourth Years of L & M

BROADLY speaking, the first two years of L & M have been considered as years of general preparatory study, designed to give the student a conception of the dynamic nature of musical material in addition to the equivalents at least of conventional two-year harmony and one-year counterpoint courses. It should be borne in mind that when we speak of L & M in terms of "years," the work of the average student is outlined; the superior student, through the flexibility of the program, may be doing work considerably more advanced. By the end of the second year the student is expected to have mastered fundamental techniques of writing and analysis and to have acquired a wide familiarity with musical repertoire of all types and periods. These are considered minimum requirements; in addition, the student will have absorbed from the individual teacher those values that can be conveyed only by free creative teaching.

Perhaps we should stress at this point our awareness that it is unrealistic to expect equal absorption or retention on the part of every student. There is a great difference between expecting a student to learn and giving him an opportunity to learn. L & M covers a great deal of ground and endeavors to develop the student's powers of apprehension and synthesis; it is not a memory course in the sense that each student is necessarily held responsible for having "learned" every detail that may have been covered during four years of intensive work. This idea of learning, viewed against opportunity of learning, becomes more significant in the later years of the curriculum. In practice, some students do not actually seem to progress very much beyond an acceptable proficiency in more or less teachable techniques such as strict counterpoint, part-writing, and simplified "formal" analysis. Not all students are equally gifted with imagination, curiosity, or intellect. As with any serious study, it is invariably the more gifted who will profit the most in L & M. It is for these reasons that we return again to our emphasis on certain minima that can reasonably be required of all students. Beyond these minima, we feel that there is no limitation to what may be learned or absorbed by the student of superior capacities and mature interests.

As a matter of making certain that the *minimum* requirements have been satisfied, uniform examinations have been given at the end of the second year to students of all L & M instructors. Such uniform examinations, it is understood, are merely one required section of a more complete final examination; the remainder of the examination is drawn up at the discretion of the individual instructor. The required uniform examination in the spring of 1951 was as follows:

1. Write a short two-part canon for violin and cello.
2. Over a figured bass (taken from Handel Concerto Grosso, Opus 6, No. 3, and given at examination time), realize a melody for flute and a part for a keyboard instrument.
3. Given a violin part (composed by a faculty member, and distributed at examination time), compose parts for two other instruments.
4. Given a cantus firmus (taken from Koechlin), write fifth species counterpoint both above and below.

Students were given one hour and a half to do three of the above four problems. Other portions of the final examination, given separately by the various instructors, were directed toward ear-training, listening, and discussion of styles; at least one portion of the examination was to be directed toward those aspects of L & M instruction and experience not easily covered by conventional examination techniques.

It has been found over several years of L & M instruction that much of the benefit derived by the student is not easily measured by written examinations. It is for this reason that the L & M faculty has adhered to the policy of designing examinations for the testing of minimum accomplishments only. On the other hand, the policy implies a very high standard (for example, the 90 percent passing grade in Basic Vocabulary) for satisfying the requirements of these examinations. For what the student accomplishes *beyond* the minimum, examinations may or may not be required by the instructor. Here again, the L & M point of view assumes, in ideal terms, that the student himself is best able to evaluate what he has derived from his study. In practical terms, frequent conferences between student and instructor help to clarify progress and accomplishment for both parties.

It should perhaps be emphasized again that the L & M faculty is bound by general agreement on objectives in terms of materials, skills, and information. Statements of objectives have been formulated, modified, and reaffirmed since the curriculum has been in operation; it is to be stressed that the idea of the curriculum remains fluid and that adjustments are constantly being made. Meetings of the L & M faculty, for the purpose of scrutinizing objectives, serve the helpful purpose of reminding individual instructors that their students may be examined by other instructors from time to time and that a common purpose must constantly illuminate the teaching of all instructors. Exchange of ideas about manners of instruction, day-to-day classroom techniques, musical materials found especially suitable, has proved stimulating and helpful to all members of the faculty. Each instructor, however, retains freedom to teach in his own way, using such materials as he sees fit and drawing on his own experience as an active and practicing musician. In the words of President Schuman, the operation of the curriculum is to be one of "organized flexibility" with emphasis on an "unencumbered, methods-free teaching relationship."

OBJECTIVES FOR END OF SECOND YEAR

As examples of objectives to be attained, covering materials and techniques, at the end of the second year, the following outline may be noted:

Form: Detailed study of
> Invention
> Madrigal, motet
> Ground bass

Introductory study of
> Sonata-allegro of the classical period
> Passacaglia
> Chaconne
> Dance suite
> Fantasia
> Toccata
> Fugue and allied styles
> Concerto grosso
> Rondo forms

Harmony: Advanced harmony; the use of harmony as a structural foundation of "classic and romantic" music; chorale harmonization

Counterpoint: Two- and three-part contrapuntal writing
> (*a*) Obbligato (cantus firmus and added voices)
> (*b*) Interdependent—simultaneous writing of two or three lines
> (*c*) Imitative—canon
> (*d*) New line, or lines, added to a given continuo (figured or unfigured)

> Rhythmic aspects of counterpoint
> Survey of species counterpoint
> Organum; faux-bourdon

Compositional devices, with special attention to those used in types of counterpoint above, such as:
> Inversion
> Retrogression
> Stretto

Assignment of thirty major works to be studied outside of class by the students (material to be drawn from all periods from the twelfth to the twentieth centuries).

REPORTS OF INSTRUCTORS—END OF
SECOND YEAR

That this outline indicates minima only may be illustrated by the following quotation from an instructor's report on a second-year class:

In this class we covered a good deal this year, I think. I began by cleaning up modulation and chorale harmonization, then proceeded to do free counterpoint, after which we took up strict counterpoint, and finally ended up with fugue writing. In fact, the home assignment for the final examination (a "thesis," if you will) was the writing of a complete three-voiced fugue, for the composing of which I gave the students over two weeks' time. Until about a month before the final examination, they had written only expositions of fugues; but, then, after numerous analyses of entire fugues in various styles, I pushed them off the deep end with, for me at least, delightful results. As I had expected, the pieces finally delivered gave a perfect picture of each personality—musical, mental, and otherwise. The whole business was very revealing, particularly in view of what must be further accomplished in that field in the third year. But even now they all know quite thoroughly at least the meaning of contrapuntal writing. They analyze very well indeed.

On the question of "intangible" values, not measurable by examination, the following passage from another instructor's report (end of second year) may be of interest:

A major accomplishment, to my mind, is the interest the students have developed in music. Where, in the early stages, the greater percentage of students had really no interest in the art form itself, now nearly all the students have a true curiosity about the art and anything pertaining to the art. A good and reasonable perspective has been developed between technique and its purpose. In only rare cases, in my experience, did the students remain in the position of wanting to learn "new chords" or the like. Eventually, some understanding of the relationship between the actual handling of musical materials and the musical values (expressiveness, or quality of music) was reached, and at the same time, for the most part, the students developed their techniques quite rapidly.

Instructors' reports such as the above are representative and give an idea of how each member of the faculty is expected to appraise his own work. The reports contain not only evaluations and accounts of procedure but also criticisms and suggestions for increasing the effectiveness of the L & M program as a whole. They constitute, also, far and above any grades that are given, valuable records and comment on the real progress and achievements of the students.

SPECIALIZED AND REPERTOIRE CLASSES

Despite the considerable disparity that exists, and will always exist, in the matter of student achievement and rate of progress, it is generally assumed that at the end of two years the student is ready for a more intensive and specialized study of materials and techniques. It has been observed by many members of the L & M faculty that students seem to show remarkable development, in terms of assimilation, in the period between the end of the second and the beginning of the third year of study. When the L & M curriculum was first organized, students were, in fact, divided into classes of specialization at the conclusion of their second year of study. Pianists, singers, players of orchestral instruments, met in groups under specialists in the various fields and concentrated further study primarily on the literatures of their own media. This division into specialized classes was abandoned at the beginning of the academic year 1952–1953, since it was felt that a more integrated over-all course was possible by having the student remain with the same L & M instructor throughout his undergraduate career. At the same time, concentration on specific repertoires has been retained through the establishment of repertoire classes for singers and pianists. Students are assigned to these only upon the recommendation of their L & M instructors that they are prepared for them, that is, ready to study and discuss repertoire with some technical and stylistic discernment. In general, such assignments are still made at the end of the second year, but the judgment of the L & M instructor is to be used in all instances. Exceptional students may be assigned to repertoire classes at the end of one year, while slower students are to be held back until they are technically equipped to cope with the work. (The repertoire classes are discussed below.)

While the pianist or singer, as the case may be, attends two one-and-one-half hour repertoire classes per week, he continues to do work with his L & M instructor at whatever stage of advancement he has reached. Specialized classes for other categories of performers have been eliminated from the curriculum, with the very important exception of the classes in Chamber Music, where much of the student's most vital musical development is achieved. Chamber music classes, especially for string players, cover many of the most interesting and important phases of repertoire. Various groups to which the student may be assigned will work on string quartets, trios, sonatas with piano, chamber ensembles with piano, or miscellaneous combinations for which literature exists. It is understood that all string players, and all pianists, will have explored some portion of this vast repertoire during their years at the School.

The repertory of important, original solo and chamber works for the woodwind, brass, and percussion instruments being limited, the students who specialize in these instruments are consequently at a disadvantage. In particular, they are deprived of the insight into musical processes which the string player and pianist or singer can scarcely avoid, since the very vastness of these respective repertoires forces the violinist or pianist into continual active performing contact with a variety of significant musical literatures.

The trombonist or drummer, in his L & M work, will in general study and analyze the same repertoire as his fellow-student violinist of equal level of advancement, but he often feels that his reactions and insights are apt to seem second-hand, since, in the case of quartets or sonatas, he is dealing with works in which the trombonist or xylophonist can seldom participate.

In recent years our brass ensembles have been greatly assisted by the revival of a large repertory of fine Renaissance chamber music, either written originally for brass or now made available in idiomatic arrangements. Arrangements of both vocal and instrumental Renaissance and baroque polyphonic music have proved most satisfactory in seeking a "serious" repertory for our ensemble class of saxophone majors, whose skill generally has scarcely any outlet at all in concert music.

The woodwind players are distributed into woodwind quintet groups, for which a usable, if not too extensive or distinguished, repertory exists. However, every effort is made to assemble the mixed, irregular groups necessary to perform the moderate repertoire of important chamber works scattered throughout the various periods and styles, which provide good workouts for an exposed clarinet, horn, trumpet, or other woodwind, or brass.

A more recent feature of L & M ensemble studies has been the formation of vocal chamber groups, for which a splendid Renaissance repertory exists. If this can be developed it might put the singer in the same advantageous position as the string player, able to make the acquaintance of both solo and ensemble repertoires by participating in their performance.

With regard to the percussion instruments, two different ensemble groups rehearse weekly under the guidance of the percussion instructors. One of these specializes in works originally scored for percussion (necessarily limited to twentieth century works); the other class studies the percussion ensemble textures in the standard symphonic repertoire. As yet neither class has been related specifically to the L & M program, except perhaps as concerns the study of twentieth century composing techniques.

All these students, in any case, continue to work with the L & M instructor, who as a rule orients studies of musical literature to meet particular needs. On the more advanced levels of L & M, study groups tend to become smaller, and the instructor usually devotes more time to individual conferences and to study projects for individual students. Class work, however, is by no means abandoned. Classes or group meetings are instituted where common purposes and needs may be served.

The idea of specialization is retained to some extent in the present L & M organization. Exchange of views with other faculties has resulted in a series of flexible requirements for different categories of performers in so far as advanced work in L & M is concerned. It is not held necessary, for example, that every singer be required to demonstrate ability at fugal writing or composition of a more than rudimentary sort. Students majoring in conducting, on the other hand, are expected to proceed intensively in composition, orchestration, and analysis, to a point of determinable utility. In cases where actual requirements are held to a minimum, as with singers, individual students may of course proceed on a voluntary basis as far as their interests and capacities will allow.

OTHER WORK WITH ADVANCED STUDENTS

The L & M instructor becomes, with his advanced students, more and more of a general musical adviser. The student's "dossier" generally takes on a more individualized character as the instructor attempts to guide the student's theoretical studies along lines most suited to the student's interest as a performer. Works are studied in greater detail, and new facets are discovered. Studies in harmony, counterpoint, form, and other structural aspects of music are pursued at a more advanced level. Writing skills such as orchestration receive greater emphasis, and performing skills such as ensemble playing and conducting are utilized with greater effectiveness. Composition is, in general, emphasized more strongly on the upper levels of L & M. Some instructors require each student to compose the equivalent of a sonata allegro for string quartet or orchestra; other instructors make the larger assignments in composition optional. In all cases, however, sufficient writing is required to demonstrate that the student fully understands the problems presented in the assignment. Attempts of this sort, even when the student lacks a creative gift, are useful aids to understanding the accomplishments of composers. The aim of writing assignments is simply that; it is not to suggest that all music students should or can become composers themselves.

In the third and fourth years, emphasis is also generally stronger on reading assignments. Juilliard School of Music has an excellent library of books on music as well as music itself, and it is the hope of every member of the L & M faculty that all students will learn to use, *on their own initiative*, the sources and facilities afforded. Although most L & M instructors, as has been suggested above, avoid recommending or requiring specific textbooks or references, they at the same time hope to encourage a habit of general reading and comparison of sources of information. A typical reading project in a third- or fourth-year L & M class may consist of the instructor's assigning to each of a number of students a book representing one view on a given subject. The students are asked to report to the class on the books they have read, to comment on them, and to exchange ideas on what may well be highly divergent approaches or presentations. It is in the nature of L & M instruction that all manner of books may be brought to the attention of students; suggestions for reading need not be limited to technical works, musical biographies and histories, or studies in style and appreciation. The "academic" section of the Juilliard library is often used by the L & M class, as well as that section officially devoted to music and to books dealing with music.

THIRD- AND FOURTH-YEAR OBJECTIVES

The general outline of objectives for the third and fourth years, approved in 1948 by the L & M faculty, may clarify the nature of studies undertaken, and is given below.

RECOMMENDED OBJECTIVES IN THIRD AND FOURTH YEARS (1948 OUTLINE)

A. GENERAL
1. More detailed knowledge of styles of periods determined by the instructor, but generally (depending on medium) covering *earlier* phases of the literature involved, in the third year of L & M, and *later* phases of the literature in the fourth year.
2. Comparison of these styles with any relevant period or media, in terms of influence, adaptation, change, or contrast.
3. Study of standard repertoire, plus guidance toward *extension* and *enlargement* of repertoire (familiar and unfamiliar music).
4. Performance of music in class must be stressed *and made possible*.

B. Specific

1. The purpose of L & M is to produce better performers. Evaluation of this result cannot be made from a purely L & M viewpoint and must, therefore, be tested in closest co-ordination with *all* major and ensemble classes.

2. The following goals should be achieved by *all* divisions of L & M, the importance of the various elements being emphasized according to their place in the specific literature:

   (*a*) acquaintance with development of smaller and larger forms;

   (*b*) acquaintance with changes in rhythmic, melodic, harmonic, and contrapuntal practices and characteristics in the periods covered and in the works of specific composers;

   (*c*) ability to prove knowledge of principles used in the above (*a* and *b*) by writing and analyzing.

This statement was later amplified in the following memorandum adopted as a general guide by the L & M faculty. In connection with this memorandum it should be noted, however, that the chronological sequence is and has been applied very loosely. Some instructors prefer a chronological approach; others take a quite definite stand against it. The same instructor, too, may change or modify his handling of material from year to year. Here again, it is not the *manner* of teaching or presentation that is prescribed; these summaries and guides have no function other than to outline in a general fashion essential material to which attention should be given at some time during the course of study.

AMPLIFIED OUTLINE FOR THIRD AND FOURTH YEARS

NOTE: The following does not apply to voice students,* since the problems of the singer are quite different from those of the instrumentalist and composer.

THIRD YEAR

Contrapuntal and harmonic practice in terms of structure and function: the Renaissance
to approximately 1830.

Compositional style: Emphasis on the state of music at the time of Bach-Handel-Couperin, with reference to preceding and succeeding periods including that of the Gabrielis, Monteverdi, Elizabethan England, Purcell, the Mannheim School, and early classical period. (Comparison with later music, especially that of today, is strongly recommended.)

Forms: Emphasis to be determined in relation to the literature for the specific interests of members of the class—piano, organ, strings, etc.

> Fantasia
> Canzona
> Ricercare
> Toccata
> Variations
> Ground bass: Early baroque
>   ground, Chaconne, Passacaglia
> The Suite: Dance forms
> Partita
> Fugue
> Motet
> Madrigal
> Recitative and aria

* See page 146, below.

> Cantata
> Opera and oratorio
> French and Italian overtures
> Chorale: prelude, variations,
>   fantasia
> Trio sonata
> Solo sonata
> Concerto grosso
> Divertimento
> Serenade
> Classical sonata, symphony,
>   concerto

Harmony and counterpoint:
> The change toward tonality
> Realization of figured bass
> Writing of at least:
>> A variation form or suite
>> First movement of a sonata allegro
>> A fugal exposition

Miscellaneous:
> Study of instrumentation of the period
> Study of the C clefs
> The changing place of music in Europe from sixteenth
> through eighteenth centuries, and effect on musical
> techniques

FOURTH YEAR

> Contrapuntal and harmonic practice in terms of
> structure and function: Beethoven to the pres-
> ent. Changing place of music—sociology,
>   esthetics, new techniques.

Form:
> Nineteenth century sonata, symphony
> Symphonic poem
> Short "characteristic" pieces
> National dance styles—waltz, mazurka, etc.

Free forms
Neo-baroque and neo-classic influences
The virtuoso etude, caprice
The sonata and symphony of today
Opera
Harmony:
Nineteenth century chromaticism
Twelve-tone writing
Chord building other than in thirds
Polychords
Polytonality
Free use of triads and sevenths
Parallelism
Revival of modes
Atonality
Other twentieth century phenomena
Counterpoint:
Contrapuntal lines suggested by harmonic chromaticism
Counterpoint as practiced by twentieth century composers
Rhythmic elements in twentieth century music; changing concepts of rhythm
Orchestration as an integral part of composition

The student is expected to write original examples illustrating the above points.

REPORTS OF INSTRUCTORS—THIRD-YEAR LEVEL

A few excerpts from instructors' reports may make clear some aspects of work pursued at about the third-year level:

I treated this class as a comparative study in instrumental music between 1580–1830, examined through the techniques which made it up. Writing assignments were spotlighted as important and spectacular. There were only two major ones —at about the tenth week, and toward the end of the year. They were to demonstrate what the student had learned in the course; the first (in the concerto grosso period) could be either in classic concerto grosso style, in which case I would judge it by period criteria, or in a contemporary idiom, in which case I would judge it as a "major composition teacher." The final assignment, started during study of the rococo symphony, covered that field with the same alternatives. The works were to be scored for the combinations available in the class; they would be rehearsed, played, analyzed, and discussed before the class as a whole.

The results were considerably better than I expected, probably because of the sense of being on display. The works were to be heard not only by the students' teacher but by their friends. To cope with this situation, it is evident that they not only looked carefully at the music they were studying in class but also called on all their musical background. A reasonably faithful concerto grosso would suddenly have eight bars of Rossini. The class would react violently, and we would find out the technical reasons why it sounded like Rossini (or Copland, or Wagner, or Palestrina). Discussing these assignments took six weeks of the course.

It is unnecessary to dilate on the technical knowledge demanded, melodic, harmonic, formal—from a scoring, transposition, notation, or stylistic viewpoint—in fulfilling this assignment. Something should be said about the way in which many alarming pitfalls in conventional "theory"— those involving rests, unisons, part-writing, tendencies of notes to resolve logically—are avoided when a player thinks of them on an instrument.

Our remaining weeks were spent in a chronological survey. A lot of attention was given to the technical reasons *why* Haydn sounds different from Mozart, or Handel from Vivaldi. An effort was made to show the direction of a composer's development, as well as the musical ecology. A list of works follows this report. Usually the major movements were analyzed in detail, and the rest of the work and any relevant outside reading were indicated. About the fourth week, I gave out a partial bibliography of reasonably reliable editions and references, requesting reports on each.

The list of works studied, and the bibliography, are appended.

MUSIC ANALYZED IN THIRD-YEAR CLASS

Prokofiev: Violin Concerto (G)
Debussy: L'Après-Midi d'un Faune
Mozart: Piano Quartet (G)
Landino: Ballata
Palestrina: Missa Papae Marcellus
Gabrieli, G.: Sonata Pian e Forte
Pezel, J.: Turm-Musik
Hassler, H.: Canzona
Rameau: Les Paladins
Fischer, J. K. F.: Le Journal de Printemps
Rosenmüller: Suite (C)
Lully: Phaeton, Overture
Corelli: Concerto Grosso (C)
Vivaldi: Concerto Grosso (D)
Handel: Concerti Grossi (B-flat, E, D)
   Water Music (Harty)
   Water Music (Gesellschaft edition)
Bach: Brandenburg Concerti (I, III, V)
  Suites (I, III)
  Toccata and Fugue (D) (Stokowski; Weinrich)
  Magnificat
  B-Minor Mass (Crucifixus et Resurrexit)
Stravinsky: Dumbarton Oaks Concerto
Barber: Capricorn Concerto
Bloch: Concerto Grosso
Pergolesi: Stabat Mater

Bach, W. F.: Concerto (Steinberg)
Bach, K. P. E.: Sonatas
Bach, J. C.: Flute Quintet (D)
Mozart: Symphonies No. 20, 29, 35, 41
　　　　Don Giovanni (Act II, Finale)
　　　　Requiem
Tchaikovsky: Symphony No. 2
Stravinsky: Symphony in Three Movements
　　　　Baiser de la Fée
Haydn: Symphonies (Farewell, Imperial, E-flat, B-flat,
　　　　London)
Beethoven: Variations, La Ci Darem La Mano
　　　　Symphonies No. 1, 2
　　　　Quartets; Opus 59, No. 3; Opus 95; Opus 131
Rossini: Gazza Ladra, Overture
Schubert: Symphonies No. 2, 5
Berlioz: Symphonie Fantastique

A PARTIAL CHECK LIST OF REFERENCES FOR THIRD- AND FOURTH-YEAR L & M CLASSES

I. SOURCES

　　Denkmäler deutscher Tonkunst
　　Denkmäler der Tonkunst in Oesterreich
　　Schering, A.: *Geschichte der Musik in Beispielen*
　　Davison-Apel: *Historical Anthology of Music*

　　The collected editions of the complete works of Vivaldi, J. S. Bach, Handel, Mozart, Beethoven, Schubert.

　　New York Public Library, in co-operation with the W.P.A., issued prior to 1940 a blueprint series of unpublished scores, including a number of symphonies by Stamitz, Cannabich, etc.

II. SECONDARY SOURCE MATERIAL

　　Bach, K. P. E.: *Versuch über die Wahre Art das Klavier zu Spielen*

　　Mozart, Leopold: *Versuch einer gründlichen Violinschule*

Quantz, J. J.: *Versuch einer Anweisung die Flöte tra-versiere zu spielen*
David-Mendel: *The Bach Reader*
Mozart, W. A.: *The Letters of Mozart and his Family* (translated and edited by Emily Anderson)
Deutsch, O. E.: *The Schubert Reader*
Nottebohm, G.: *Ein Skizzenbuch von Beethoven*

III. GENERAL (in English)
Lang, Paul Henry: *Music in Western Civilization*
Nef, Karl: *An Outline of the History of Music*
Reese, Gustave: *Music in the Middle Ages*
Bukofzer, Manfred: *Music in the Baroque Era*
Einstein, Alfred: *Music in the Romantic Era*
Slonimsky, Nicholas: *Music Since 1900* (up to 1937)
Allen, W. D.: *Philosophies of Music History*
Bekker, Paul: *The Story of the Orchestra*
Sachs, Curt: *The History of Musical Instruments*

IV. DICTIONARIES AND ENCYCLOPEDIAS
Baker: *Biographical Dictionary of Music and Musicians*
Apel, Willi: *Harvard Dictionary of Music*
Oxford History of Music
Thompson, Oscar: *International Cyclopedia of Music and Musicians*
Cobbett, W. W.: *Cyclopedic Survey of Chamber Music*
Catalog of the Edwin A. Fleisher Collection of the Philadelphia Free Library

V. PERIODICALS
The Musical Quarterly (G. Schirmer)
Music and Letters (London)
Notes (Music Library Association, Library of Congress)
Modern Music (League of Composers, New York)

VI. BIOGRAPHIES, SPECIAL STUDIES
Spitta, P.: *Bach* (published 1873–1880)
Schweitzer, A.: *Johann Sebastian Bach* (published 1905–1912)
Terry, C. S.: *Bach, A Biography* (published 1928)

Bach's Orchestra
Johann Christian Bach, A Biography
Flower, Newman: *George Frideric Handel*
Geiringer, Karl: *Haydn, A Creative Life in Music*
Einstein, Alfred: *Mozart, His Character, His Work*
Dent, E. J.: *Mozart's Operas, A Critical Study*
Thayer, A.: *The Life of Ludwig van Beethoven*
Abraham, Gerald: *The Music of Schubert*

Another instructor's report, covering similar ground in the third year of L & M, may be compared as to manner of approach and techniques of teaching:

Music selected for study:
Instrumental music of the baroque period (first semester)
Instrumental music of the early classical period (second semester)
Analysis:
Both familiar and unfamiliar music of the period are used to furnish examples for analysis.

1. Texture
2. Linear-melodic features
3. Tonality
4. Harmonic features
5. Contrapuntal features
6. Dynamics
7. Phrasing, articulation
8. Rhythmic characteristics
9. Structure
10. Use of instruments

These categories are used for a detailed examination of each musical example.

The intention is not merely a *description* of the chords, rhythmic patterns, intervals, etc., but rather an effort to discover the *purpose* behind the particular musical constituents found, and their interaction upon each other.

Harmonic, contrapuntal theory:

Once the harmonic and contrapuntal vocabulary in a given style has been isolated, the theory and grammar which may be formulated from it are studied in textbooks (such as Piston's) but only in so far as these formulations bear specifically on the music being studied at the time.

Composing:

At this point, the students write original compositions in the style being studied, for *combinations* of instruments characteristic of the period. All music is performed in class by the students themselves, not only when complete but also *in the process of being written*, a little at a time, whatever the students are able to get written. These pieces are not considered exercises; we try to make them personal expressions, but from the viewpoint of the eighteenth century, not the twentieth. The intention is to comprehend the esthetic quality and the vocabulary of a past period as understood during its own day.

General objective:

To develop a practical, working technique for investigating any given piece of music. The first stage of this is to acquire facility in locating and accurately describing all external characteristics (as in the ten categories indicated above).

Then, using only the music itself as evidence, to try to get at its essence as communication, to understand these and similar points:

1. Interaction of all technical features, one upon the other, and relation of all to the composite whole.
2. Limitations and possibilities of the particular vocabulary found.
3. Extent of consistency and variability in the particular technical phenomena observed.
4. Question of proportion between clichés, more or less

established sound formulas, and free invention in each case.

Also in 1, 2, 3, and 4:

(*a*) Why?

(*b*) What result?

Students:

The above represents the procedures followed in my present class. Obviously it depends for much of its effectiveness on the student's ability to *read fluently and boldly at sight on his own instrument*. The most hampered in this respect seem to be pianists and singers. Also missing is a bold, experimental attitude toward improvising (in the style being studied) on one's own instrument.

Students who have studied piano as an auxiliary instrument seldom make full use of the quite adequate if limited facility they have acquired because of this apparent lack of trained facility in reading and improvising.

This puts an obstacle in the way of investigating a large amount of music freely and independently. Many students rely on recordings for this, which I believe is often a mistake because the student is apt to take many details for granted when they go by smoothly on a record. Recordings are not suitable for the minute scrutiny of a short phrase or a single bar, which is so often indispensable.

On the positive side, the multiple approach of playing-analyzing-composing in investigating a given musical style has frequent good results. Many students come to acquire a working articulate understanding of musical processes in terms of craft or "stylistic know-how" rather than dogma or mysticism.

These summaries give a fair idea of the inclusiveness and scope of subject matter on an average third-year level. Choice of repertoire studied differs extensively but is, in all cases, wide and varied. Music history is thus clearly understood, not merely as a matter of names and dates and verbal descriptions of "style" and "form"; orchestration is examined in context and is practiced creatively; conducting is begun (under the guidance of the instructor) with the stimulating opportunity of making an ensemble perform one's own work. Creative application of everything learned, on a cumulative basis, is constantly encouraged, with the insistence that the student be occupied not with harmony, or with counterpoint, or with orchestration, but with music. The imaginative student is given scope for almost any enterprise he wishes to undertake. In most classes on the third- or fourth-year levels, individual "projects" are given every encouragement. Occasionally these projects are assigned, but often they develop from the student's initiative. An example may be taken from another instructor's report:

One of the most rewarding "projects" undertaken in my present "advanced" class was entirely the result of a student's interest and initiative; I really did nothing but give him encouragement. The student's project was the orchestration of Schoenberg's piano pieces, Opus 19. He had learned them thoroughly; although not a piano major, he was able to play them from memory. His purpose was to orchestrate the pieces as he thought Schoenberg might have done. Over a period of weeks, he studied intensively many of the early and "middle-period" works of Schoenberg, with a great deal of penetration. He derived an excellent idea of the historical relation of Schoenberg to Wagner, Brahms, Bruckner, and Mahler, and drew a number of interesting conclusions. The orchestration itself, for a large combination of instruments, was brilliant and quite Schoenbergian in sound. The student conducted the performance for the large class (after the pieces had first been played on the piano by another student), gave a little lecture, and set off a lively discussion. Not only did the student learn a good deal, but the entire class was greatly stimulated.

The projects undertaken by third- and fourth-year students range from early music to contemporary and cover a variety of interests. Some may be directed toward advanced contrapuntal study, others toward problems in the evolution of tonality, still others toward orchestration, prosody, or other facets of creative technique. Many projects are of a comparative nature: the student may undertake side-by-side analyses of the Mozart C Minor Serenade and the Stravinsky Octet, or compare fugues of Bach, Mozart, and Hindemith. The results of projects undertaken may be presented either through written papers or, more usually, by performance and discussion of the material involved. Many projects undertaken in advanced L & M classes have shown great imagination and skill, and a number of the best papers written by students have been retained in the files of the department.

SPECIALIZED CLASSES ON THIRD- AND FOURTH-YEAR LEVELS

A. Voice

It has been suggested above that requirements are made somewhat flexible according to the major interests of given students. Originally, it was planned that the L & M curriculum should be approximately the same for all students of the school. Trial on this basis, however, provided convincing evidence that this plan was not entirely practicable, especially with regard to students majoring in voice, and more particularly with regard to those voice students enrolled in the Opera Department.

Entering voice students are assigned to L & M instructors precisely as are other students. The primary responsibility of the L & M instructor is to see that the voice student masters the "Basic Vocabulary" and acquires some notions of general musical repertoire. The voice student will, in general, remain under the guidance of the L & M instructor for two years of basic instruction, or until such time as he can completely satisfy the instructor as to the following:

1. Thorough knowledge of:
    (*a*) scales (major and minor)—recognize on paper
    (*b*) triads
    (*c*) seventh chords, suspensions, anticipations
    (*d*) vocabulary of musical terms
2. Ability to:
    (*a*) explain the logic of a modulation (by substitution of chord names)
    (*b*) reduce an altered chord to its unaltered state
    (*c*) play the correct chords of a piano part of a song on the piano
    (*d*) analyze form by noticing repetition of large or small elements
    (*e*) sing accurately on syllable *la* (without pitch) the rhythm of a first violin part in a Haydn adagio, with many sixteenth and thirty-second notes
    (*f*) read accurately at sight an average. little-

known song of Schumann, Franz, or Schubert (without words, but in rhythm)

When these requirements have been satisfied, the student may be recommended by the L & M instructor for
the specialized classes in Vocal Repertoire, which will
make up the principal area of classroom work for the following two years of his course. The student will, however, remain nominally assigned to the L & M teacher,
who will continue to function as his adviser and who will
be responsible for the student's progress. The student
may, at his option, or on the advice of the L & M teacher,
pursue further technical studies or other work in L & M,
although intensive further work is not required. In most
cases, the voice student is expected to continue in L & M
to the extent of becoming more familiar with non-vocal
literature and of participating in such vocal ensemble performances as the L & M teacher may direct.

Students in the Opera Theatre, because of the great demands upon their time, involving daily rehearsals in the
manner of a repertory opera company, are excused from
all further L & M study except the classes in Vocal Repertoire. These students, consequently, do not receive full
"credit" for L & M at the rate of eight points per semester.
Their records show three points per semester, based on
the three hours weekly spent in the Vocal Repertoire
classes.

In Vocal Repertoire I, attention is centered on German
Lieder, principally Schubert, Schumann, Brahms, and
Wolf. Some one hundred and fifty songs of these com-
posers are performed in class and studied in detail. The

students are required to purchase all material so used. The procedures in Vocal Repertoire I are described as follows by the instructor:

For a given class meeting each student is assigned one song which he is supposed to

1. translate literally into English;
2. present (text) in a condensed version in idiomatic English;
3. analyze musically as to
   (*a*) form,
   (*b*) chordal background,
   (*c*) relationship between the vocal and instrumental parts;
4. play on the piano: most important harmonic progressions, leaving out pianistic figuration;
5. sing in class.

This procedure demands some lecturing on my part, depending on the problems discovered in performance. Most of such "lecturing" is of the technical or analytical sort, with some history and poetry thrown in when necessary. Discussion is encouraged but not on questions pertaining to esthetics. About one hour of each session is devoted to analysis and performance. We averaged six performances by six students of three assigned songs (per session). This means that each student acquires first-hand performing knowledge of some fifty songs. Records were used seldom, mostly of symphonic or chamber music. Hardly any written work seems necessary. Most of our technical work was illustrated by the students at the blackboard. Many wrote songs, but this, although encouraged, was not demanded.

Vocal Repertoire II classes are conducted in the same manner. The course covers an approximately equal number (150) of songs and airs ranging in period from the Elizabethan and the Baroque to the contemporary. Students in this class are not required to purchase all the material used, because of the expense involved, but are expected to obtain the material through a judicious combination of their own resources and those of the library. Since vocal works of Mozart and songs of the Italian masters are generally so well-covered in private voice lessons, these are not emphasized in any Vocal Repertoire classes. A sample of work to be covered by a given individual student during the second year may be indicated by the following list:

10 songs by Elizabethan composers
6 by Purcell
3 each of Bach, Handel, Rameau, Lully, Gluck, Grétry
10 by Gabriel Fauré
8 by Debussy
3 each of Chausson, Duparc, Ravel, Poulenc
4 by contemporary English or American composers

Since each student in the class is responsible for an equivalent group of works, the class as a whole is able to cover a broad range of repertoire and to acquire a useful foundation upon which to build. No formal examinations are given in the Vocal Repertoire classes. The student's almost daily participation and the nature of this participation enable the instructor to arrive at an accurate evaluation of the student's progress and accomplishments. The instructor's grade in the course is turned over to the student's L & M adviser, who notes it in the "dossier" as shown in Appendix 2.

B. Piano

Special classes in L & M for pianists have been held since the L & M program was inaugurated. The emphasis has shifted somewhat during the past few years, but the essential purpose has remained: that of giving the piano student a comprehensive view of keyboard literature in terms of musical techniques. Four instructors have been involved with these classes since the curriculum was instituted. As with general L & M instruction, each of these teachers has been free to devise his own methods and approaches for his own classes; here, too, the instructors are guided by general aims formulated by the L & M faculty as a whole.

Piano students are required to continue with regular L & M studies while enrolled in the special repertoire classes. Assignment to repertoire classes is made only upon recommendation of the L & M instructor-adviser; as has been stated above, the student is generally, although not invariably, prepared for these classes at the end of two years. The repertoire classes in piano are considered a supplement to the regular L & M study, rather than a direct continuation of the first two years. Techniques of writing, attention to non-keyboard repertoire, and the pursuit of other aspects of L & M study remain in the province of the principal L & M teacher.

The Piano Repertoire classes, like those in Vocal Repertoire, constitute a two-year sequence. Students as a rule study under the same instructor in Piano Repertoire I and II, although this is not mandatory. The advantages of gaining the points of view of two instructors may be weighed against the advantages of a continuous two-year course with one instructor. Here a matter of educational policy is involved: it is possible in principle to "learn" as much (in the event of overlapping with two instructors) from studying one work with two teachers as from studying two works with one teacher. We feel that the student should, by his third year in L & M, be given a certain freedom of choice.

The classes in Piano Repertoire may be conducted on a chronological basis or not; but in any case they embrace a survey of keyboard literature from roughly 1600 to the present day. In some instances the two-year study has been divided into a study of the more familiar repertoire during the first year (Bach through Brahms), and a study of earlier music and contemporary compositions in the second year. No order of study is invariable. In the two years, however, the student makes a study of many representative keyboard works that supplements the repertoire he prepares for performance with his individual piano teacher.

REPORTS OF INSTRUCTORS—PIANO
REPERTOIRE I AND II

Excerpts from reports of two instructors are given below, to show examples of specific procedures in representative classes.

Instructor A:

I. PURPOSES OF THE COURSES:

(*a*) To make a general survey of piano literature

(*b*) To improve the sight-reading ability of the individual student by requiring performance in class of works, with a minimum of outside preparation

(*c*) To analyze the works performed, covering the following points:

1. Form
2. Distinctive harmonic situations
3. Distinctive melodic situations
4. Distinctive rhythmic situations
5. Types of contrapuntal writing
6. Keyboard treatment, including piano resonance, chord spacing, types of accompaniment, pedal effects, technical requirements
7. Devices of development and variation
8. Influences on the composer
9. Problems of performance

(*d*) To develop the ability to recognize the style of a specific composer, period, or form by hearing or examining a score

(*e*) To develop articulate musicians through class discussion, especially spontaneous criticism of new or unfamiliar works

The course was planned as a series of studies of the development of various forms or types of keyboard music. The first year traced the growth and change of dance-forms, suites, character-pieces, and variations. The second year covered virtuoso pieces and etudes and the piano sonata.

This plan was employed simply for "dramatic" reasons, since it was felt that straight chronology becomes monotonous throughout the year. In the courses, a contemporary example of the form to be surveyed was performed, and then flash-back technique was utilized by jumping back to the period of origin of the form and tracing its development and change up to the present day. This process required from three weeks (as in the dance pieces) to ten weeks (the sonata) for the separate forms. Emphasis was on lesser-known works of the repertoire in order to give some indication that the pianist's repertoire need not be limited to those works heard year in and year out.

1. *Lectures:* Informal lectures of a general and historical nature were used throughout the courses to provide continuity, to set the stage for performance and discussion. Technical and analytical lectures were used as postscripts to material which the students had presented or to give the students a working basis in principles which were new to them (twelve-tone system, Stravinsky treatment of tonality, etc.)

2. *Assignments:* Assignments were almost entirely performance assignments for class. The few written assignments (harmonic and formal analysis, term paper) were discussed with the students in private conference.

3. *Analysis of selected works:* The course was based on analyses (some detailed, some sketchy) of selected works, most of which were live performances by students, instructor, and occasional guest artists. A few records were used, when media other than piano were discussed or when the piano works were of great difficulty and not practicable for student performance (Ives' Concord Sonata, Ravel's Scarbo, etc.).

4. *Listening:* Listening was the basis of the class discussion and analysis. Students were given the option of following a performance with or without scores.

5. *Arguing, etc.:* Class method was basically conversational, the instructor attempting to act as mediator or as one protagonist of a controversy.

6. *Performances:* Performances were almost wholly by students. Works to be performed throughout the year were

all assigned during the first week of the course to ensure adequate preparation.

II. MATERIALS USED:

No text was required for the course. It was suggested that students purchase Davison and Apel's *Historical Anthology of Music* (Harvard University Press) and Willi Apel's *Masters of the Keyboard* (Harvard University Press) because these contained many works which would be referred to or performed in class. A short general bibliography of works on keyboard music was given at the first class meeting. Other books or articles were mentioned when discussing specific composers or styles.

III. MUSIC PERFORMED IN THE COURSES INCLUDED:

Works marked with an asterisk were heard on records.

PIANO REPERTOIRE I

Dances:

Anon. Estampie (fourteenth century)

    Alta (sixteenth century)

    Dompe (sixteenth century)

    Pavanne and Galliard (seventeenth century)

    Bransle (seventeenth century)

    German dances (seventeenth century)

Hans Neusiedler: Judentanz

Byrd: Alman, Coranto, Gigue

Gibbons: Pavane

Schubert: 7 Waltzes

Weber: Polonaise (E major)

    Invitation to the Dance

Chopin: Waltz (A-flat major, Opus 42)

    Polonaise (D minor)

    Polonaise (F-sharp minor)

    Polonaise, Fantaisie

    7 Mazurkas

Liszt: Soirée de Vienne, No. 6

    2 Czardas

Smetana: Hulan

Chambonnières: Allemande
d'Anglebert: Allemande
Rameau: Menuets
J. S. Bach: 3 Minuets
　　　　　3 Klavierstücke in Suitenform
Graun: Gigue (B-flat minor)
Mozart: Minuet (D major)
　　　　Gigue (G major)
W. F. Bach: Polonaise (E-flat major)

Brahms: 3 Waltzes
　　　　2 Sarabandes
Granados: Spanish Dance
Ravel: Valses Nobles et Sentimentales
Satie: Gymnopédie
Scriabin: Mazurka (F-sharp major)
　　　　　Quasi-valse

Milhaud: 4 Saudades do Brasil
Honegger: Danse
Prokofiev: Gavotte (G minor)
Bartók: Rumanian Dance, Opus 8
　　　　3 Bulgarian Dances

Suites:

François Couperin: Les Bacchanales
Froberger: Suite (A minor)
Pachelbel: Suite (E-flat major)
Fischer: Suite (A major)
J. S. Bach: French Suite (D minor)
　　　　　English Suite (E minor)
　　　　　Partita (E minor)
　　　　　French Overture
　　　　　Overture (F major)
Handel: Suite (A major)
　　　　Suite (F minor)
Mozart: Overture in the style of Handel
Bargiel: Suite (G minor) (excerpts)

Grieg: Suite, Aus Holbergs Zeit
Debussy: Pour le piano
Ravel: Le Tombeau de Couperin
Bartók: Little Suite (1936)
Hindemith: Suite (1922)
Stravinsky: Serenade in A
Schoenberg: Suite, Opus 25 (excerpts)
Roy Harris: Piano Suite
Original suites by three students

Variations:

Luis de Narvaez: Diferencias
Cabezon: Diferencias
Peter Phillips: Coloration of Lassus' *Bon jour, mon coeur*
Hugh Aston: Hornpipe
John Munday: Goe from My Window
Sweelinck: Mein junges Leben hat ein End
Frescobaldi: Canzona, No. 2
François Couperin: Rossignol en amour
J. S. Bach: Aria variata alla italiana (Goldberg varia-
      tions) *
Handel: Chaconne (G major)
Mozart: Ah, vous dirai-je, maman
          Ein Weib ist das herrlichste Ding
Haydn: Variations (F minor) *
Beethoven: Veni amore
              Variations (E-flat major, Opus 35)
              Diabelli Variations *
Mendelssohn: Variations sérieuses
Chopin: Variations on a German tune
Liszt: Weinen, Klagen, Sorgen, Zagen
Brahms: Variations on an original theme (Opus 21)
Copland: Variations

Character-pieces:

Martin Peerson: Fall of a Leaf
Giles Farnaby: His Dream

François Couperin: Les Folies Françaises
Froberger: Lamentation
Marin Marais: Romance
K. P. E. Bach: Rondo (B-flat major)
Mozart: Adagio (B minor)
Mendelssohn: 5 Songs without Words
Schumann: Davidsbündler Dances, Opus 6
        Fantasy Pieces, Opus 111
Chopin: Nocturne, F major, Opus 15
     Nocturne, E-flat major, Opus 55
     Nocturne, B major, Opus 62
Liszt: Petrarca Sonnet (E major)
    Second Elegy
    Trauergondel (two versions)
Brahms: Intermezzo, Opus 119, No. 2
     Intermezzo, Opus 76, No. 6
     Capriccio, Opus 76, No. 1
     Capriccio, Opus 76, No. 5
     Capriccio, Opus 116, No. 3
MacDowell: At an Old Trysting Place
Fauré: Tenth Barcarolle
Beethoven: Bagatelles, Opus 33
      Bagatelles, Opus 119
      Bagatelles, Opus 126
John Field: Nocturne (B-flat major)
Schubert: Impromptu (A-flat major)
      Moment Musical (A-flat major)
      Abschied von der Erde (declamation and
      piano)
Satie: Trois Valses d'un précieux dégoûté
    Véritables Préludes Flasques
    Descriptions Automatiques
Scriabin: 4 Preludes, Opus 11
      Poème, Opus 32, No. 1
      Désir
      Masque
      5 Preludes, Opus 74

Prokofiev: Sarcasme, No. 3
Schoenberg: 6 Little Pieces, Opus 19
Honegger: 7 Short Pieces
Poulenc: Nocturne (C major)
Shostakovitch: Prelude, No. 17
Chavez: Solo
     36
Bergsma: 3 Fantasies
Bowles: 6 Preludes
Rachmaninoff: Prelude, Opus 23, No. 4
Debussy: Hommage à Rameau

PIANO REPERTOIRE II

Virtuoso pieces:
Merulo: Toccata
Frescobaldi: Toccata (F major)
Buxtehude: Toccata (E major)
François Couperin: Tic-toc-choc
J. S. Bach: Toccata (G major)
          Toccata (D major)
          Toccata (E minor)
          Toccata (F-sharp minor)
          12 Preludes, Well-Tempered Clavier
Rameau: Les Cyclopes
Scarlatti: 12 Sonatas
Mozart: Variations, Lison Dormait
Beethoven: Polonaise
Czerny: Toccata
Weber: Momento Capriccioso
Schumann: Toccata
Chopin: Allegro de Concert
Liszt: Grand Galop Chromatique
     Russian Galop
     Hungarian Rhapsody, No. 17
Balakirev: Islamey *
Albeniz: Triana
         Fête-dieu en Seville *

Debussy: L'Ile Joyeuse
Ravel: Scarbo *
Prokofiev: Toccata
Bartók: The Chase
Talma: Toccata

Etudes:

Durante: Studio (A major)
Clementi: 2 Etudes, Gradus ad Parnassum
Cramer: 2 Etudes
Czerny: 2 Etudes, Opus 740
Moscheles: 2 Etudes
Mendelssohn: 3 Etudes, Opus 104
Schumann: Paganini Etude, Opus 3
     Paganini Etude, Opus 10
Henselt: Etude, Opus 2
Chopin: 12 Etudes, Opus 10
   12 Etudes, Opus 25
Debussy: 12 Etudes (excerpts)
Szymanowski: 12 Etudes, Opus 33 (excerpts)
Bartók: 3 Etudes, Opus 18
Liszt: Paganini Etude
  12 Transcendental Etudes (three versions) (excerpts)
  Ab Irato
Alkan: Le Festin d'Esope
Rubinstein: Etude
Moszkowski: 2 Etudes
MacDowell: 12 Etudes, Opus 39
    Concert Etude
Liapounov: Carillon
Saint-Saëns: Etude in Thirds, Opus 111
Scriabin: Etudes, Opus 8, Opus 42
   Etudes in 5th, Opus 65
Prokofiev: Etude, Opus 2
Martinu: 2 Etudes
Virgil Thomson: 12 Etudes (excerpts)

Sonatas:

Kuhnau: Sonata (D major)
   Biblical Sonata (David and Goliath)
   Biblical Sonata (The Melancholy Saul)
J. S. Bach: Sonata (D major)
Scarlatti: 4 Sonatas
Galuppi: Sonata (D major)
K. P. E. Bach: Sonata (G major)
    Sonata (A-flat major)
Haydn: Sonata (E-flat major)
   Sonata (E minor)
Mozart: Sonata (B-flat major), K.281
   Sonata (B-flat major), K.333
Clementi: Sonata (B minor)
   Sonata (G minor)
Beethoven: Sonata (A major), Opus 2
   Sonata (F major), Opus 54
   Sonata (A major), Opus 101
Mendelssohn: Sonata (B-flat major)
Weber: Sonata (C major)
   Sonata (E minor) (excerpts)
Schubert: Sonata (A major), Opus 120
   Sonata (C minor)
Schumann: Sonata (F-sharp minor)
   Sonata (F minor)
Chopin: Sonata (B-flat minor)
Liszt: Sonata (B minor) *
Brahms: Sonata (F minor)
   Sonata (F-sharp minor)
Scriabin: Sonata, No. 5
   Sonata, No. 9
Griffes: Sonata
Copland: Sonata
Ives: Concord Sonata *
Poulenc: Sonata, four hands
Bartók: Sonata

Hindemith: Sonata, No. 3
Chavez: Sonatina
Original sonatas, sonatinas, or sonata-allegro movements
　　by nine students.

*Records used (in addition to those indicated by asterisk
above)*:

J. S. Bach: Passacaglia in C Minor
Mozart: Notte e giorno faticar (Don Giovanni)
　　　　　String Quartet, C Major (excerpts)
Beethoven: Third Symphony (fourth movement)
Schubert: Death and the Maiden
　　　　　The Erlking
J. S. Bach: Clavier Concerto, F minor
Roy Harris: Third Symphony (excerpts)
Schoenberg: Pierrot Lunaire (excerpts)
Bartók: Sonata (two pianos and percussion) (excerpts)

IV. FINAL EXAMINATIONS:

No final examination was given in either course. Each student chose his own term project after consultation with the instructor. Work was begun in November so that the final result would not be a hastily prepared paper or composition. The range of subjects of the research papers included:

(*a*)　An analysis of Hindemith's Ludus Tonalis
(*b*)　A comparison of the keyboard styles of K. P. E.
　　　　Bach, Mozart, and Haydn
(*c*)　The piano sonatas of W. F. Rust
(*d*)　An analysis of Ives' "Concord Sonata"
(*e*)　The influence of vocal music on keyboard music in
　　　　the nineteenth century
(*f*)　Changing standards of keyboard performance
(*g*)　The contrasting use of modal harmony in the piano
　　　　music of Fauré, Bartók, Roy Harris
(*h*)　A study of Brahms' variation technique
(*i*)　Analysis of the Schoenberg Piano Pieces, Opus 11,
　　　　Opus 19, Opus 23
(*j*)　Comparison of Bach and Handel suites

Instructor B:

PLAN OF STUDY:

To carry the study of the piano literature from the pre-classic masters as far forward as time would permit. In order not to put off the study of contemporary music to a few closing sessions, the instructor decided to devote one session in three (every Monday) to a consideration of contemporary works. In actual practice this became somewhat flexible, so that if reasonable continuity demanded two or three consecutive sessions on a contemporary work, the instructor followed the interests and needs of all concerned. There were, however, two main streams of study pursued throughout the semester.

As originally planned, the two streams were:
  I. K. P. E. Bach, Mozart, Haydn
      Beethoven, Schubert, Schumann
      Liszt, Brahms
  II. Bartók, Schoenberg, Hindemith
      Stravinsky, Ravel
      Debussy, Americans, Russians

In actual practice this proved to be much too much material for fruitful consideration. The following works were intensively studied by the students and instructor:

K. P. E. Bach:
    Sonata in A (Prussian Sonatas, 1742)
    Rondo in G
    Free Fantasy in C
Haydn:
    Sonata in A flat (complete)
    Sonata in B (last two movements)
Mozart:
    Sonatas in F, A, B flat (first movements)
    Fantasy and Fugue in C
    Rondo in A
    Gigue in G
    Minuet in D

Fantasy in C Minor (before the Sonata)
Variations on "Salve tu Domine" and "Ah, vous dirai-je"
Fantasy in F (four hands)
Sonata in F (four hands) (last movement)

Beethoven:

First movements of Opus 2, No. 3; Opus 53; and Opus 111

Slow movements of Opus 7, Opus 26, and Opus 53

Last movement of Opus 111

Eroica variation of Opus 35 studied in detail along with last movement of Eroica Symphony

Bagatelles, Opus 126 (complete)

Schubert:

Sonata in A (posthumous) (slow movement and last movement)

Sonata in B flat (posthumous) (slow movement)

Four-hand works: March in C; Lebensstürme (Allegro in A minor); Variations in A flat; Dances; Moment Musical No. 1

Liszt:

Funerailles
Mephisto Waltz
Petrarch Sonnet No. 104

Parallel with above, the following contemporary works were dealt with:

Bartók:

15 Hungarian Peasant Songs
Improvisations, Opus 20
Sonata (complete)
Outdoors Suite (complete)

Schoenberg:

Opus 11, Nos. 1 and 2
Opus 19 complete
Walzer, Opus 23
Opus 33a

The latter part of the class time was devoted completely to the performance and discussion of contemporary works prepared independently by each of the students, this latter constituting one aspect of the final examinations. All works were performed for the entire class so that each student heard approximately thirty new pieces and contributed his own mite to the development of the group as a whole. These were:

Bartók: Mikrokosmos Pieces from Vol. IV
　　　　　Suite, Opus 14
Debussy: Several Preludes, Book II
　　　　　Etudes ("pour les quarts," "pour les huits doigts")
Ravel: Gaspard de la Nuit (complete); Sonatine
Chavez: Two Preludes
Shostakovitch: Two Preludes
Hindemith: Interludii and Fugues from the "Ludus Tonalis"
　　　　　"Nachstück" and "Boston" from 1922 Suite
Prokofiev: Sonatas Nos. 3 and 7
Stravinsky: Serenade in A (two movements)
Ives: "Alcotts" from the "Concord Sonata"
Ben Weber: Piano Suite
Berg: Sonata, Opus 1

Each student was provided with the bibliographies on the two contemporary composers who received special consideration. The instructor plans to expand this in future sessions to include a sizable slice from the contemporary repertoire.

Students were asked to purchase all contemporary music studied whenever possible.

ASSIGNMENTS:

Performance: All works studied were performed in class either by the instructor or students. Recordings were used only once (a recording by Busoni of a Liszt Rhapsody).

Playing assignments were voluntary and well spaced to avoid overloading students. Examples:

>Exposition of Bartók Sonata—two weeks preparation
>Mozart: Rondo in A—several weeks
>Schoenberg: Opus 11, No. 1—one month
>Schubert: Four-hand Allegro—one month

All students were urged to read and study works under consideration before class discussion took place (no check made on this).

Generally, the level of class performance amounted to good sight-reading or rough preparation; in some cases it was of a high order; in a very few, of poor quality.

By common assent, one of the major benefits derived by the students was the opportunity to hear players of various teachers function before the group.

REPORTS:

Individual students reported on pertinent books and articles from time to time. These included:

>K. P. E. Bach: "Essay on the True Art of Playing Keyboard Instruments"
>Bartók: Hungarian Folk Music
>Leibowitz: Schoenberg et son École (Introduction)
>Articles on the piano works of Haydn and Mozart

Every student submitted a lengthy study on some contemporary piano music as part of his final examination requirements. These were close analytical, stylistic discussions designed to demonstrate how well the student had grasped the approach projected by the instructor. In some cases, the results were quite amazing; in others, merely satisfactory; in a few, disappointing. Topics included:

>Ravel: Gaspard de la Nuit
>Sonatine
>Bartók: Volume IV of the Mikrokosmos

> Sonata No. 2 for Violin and Piano
> Sonata for Two Pianos and Percussion (first
> · movement)
> Concerto No. 3 for Piano

Villa Lobos: Cycle of pieces for piano
Schoenberg: Opus 23, Nos. 1 and 2 (detailed analysis)
          Opus 19, Opus 11, No. 1 (detailed analysis)
Medtner: Piano pieces (Vergessene Weisen)
Debussy: Etudes
          Preludes
Ives: "Emerson" from "Concord Sonata"
Prokofiev: Comparative studies of several sonatas
Hindemith: Comparative study of several piano pieces
Mussorgsky: Elaborate study of the "Pictures"
Milhaud: Piano Sonata

Orientation for these term projects was careful, well prepared in advance and demanding in content. Topics were chosen by common agreement of student and teacher, and problems in handling of material were thought out in advance. All papers were submitted early enough to leave the closing weeks of the session free for the performance aspects of the examination.

READING:

Students were asked, from time to time, to consult certain articles, do some dictionary work, or read sections of authoritative studies in connection with the music under consideration.

ANALYSIS:

Specific assignments in analysis were given to individuals and to the entire group. These analyses were not text bookish in nature and were consistently tested against problems in actual performance of the material.

Essentially the main point stressed was that the performer must approach every work new to him with absolutely no preconceived ideas, that he must search for the continuity and character of the ideas as projected by the composer (whether he be Mozart or Bartók), and that his analysis must adapt itself to problems dealt with by the composer.

No analysis was considered pertinent, and no terminology was demanded, which was not intimately bound up with playing the music.

CLASS PROCEDURE:

Usually conformed to the pattern: playing, talking, planning. In a few rare instances, there was some lecturing, e.g., one full session by the instructor on the Conversation Books of Beethoven. Minutes of all classes were taken by secretaries rotating among the student group. All minutes were retained by the instructor.

OTHER SPECIALIZED CLASSES RELATED TO
L & M

The L & M curriculum is flexible enough to take care of nearly all demands of the undergraduate student, including occasional very specialized interests. In former years (prior to 1952–1953), a few specialized courses were offered on an elective basis; these included, besides conducting and orchestration, courses in Functional Music, Preparation and Editing of Manuscripts, and Composition (as a minor subject). These have all been absorbed into the general content of L & M. Attention is given these aspects of study in terms of the student's interests or needs. In some cases, the student's L & M teacher-adviser may arrange to have the student work with another member of the L & M faculty who is especially qualified in the subject in question, or who may have a group working at a particular problem. Such exchanges of students may be worked out freely by agreement among instructors and students and may be made for a specified or an indeterminate period. Thus, a student particularly interested in music for the modern dance may be assigned to work, for a given period, with an instructor whose experience in that field is more extensive than that of the student's regular instructor. Other examples of similar nature may easily be adduced.

On a graduate level, a number of specialized courses are offered, and these are occasionally open to exceptionally qualified undergraduates. Many of these courses were formerly classified as adjuncts to the L & M curriculum and were described in the school catalog as L & M VI to L & M XX. As in many universities, each course is not necessarily given each year. The following graduate courses are now (or have been) offered at Juilliard:

Musicology
Seminar in Renaissance Music
Seminar in Baroque Music
Gregorian Chant
History and Analysis of Piano Literature (Graduate)
Coaching Vocal Repertoire
History and Analysis of the Sonata
The Fugue from Bach to the Present Day
The Choral Music of J. S. Bach
Problems in Ensemble Playing and Writing
Seminar in Music Criticism
Teaching the Literature and Materials of Music

Requirements vary for admission to these courses. In many, permission of the instructor is required, or the fulfillment of specified prerequisites. Some are, of course, limited to students of voice or piano. Since all offer a continuation, in some kind, of work touched upon in undergraduate L & M, undergraduates seeking admission to these classes must demonstrate their proficiency in all appropriate areas, as well as their conversance with repertoire. The courses listed above may all be pursued as leading to the Postgraduate diploma or Master of Science degree. Graduates of other schools seeking to enroll in courses of study leading to the Master's degree or Postgraduate diploma are required to take a qualifying examination for advanced standing. This examination is similar to the graduation examination in L & M and consists of a written examination and interview (oral examination) by members of the L & M faculty.

The courses listed above are given, for the most part, by regular members of the L & M faculty. They require no special explanation, except for the course on Teaching the Literature and Materials of Music. This course is not a "methods" class but an orientation for graduate students who desire to learn more about the point of view of the School concerning the L & M curriculum and to become further acquainted with techniques and approaches used by various instructors. Although no requirement has been formulated by the School, applicants for Teaching Fellowships (see Appendix 1) have generally been enrolled in this course. Members of the class are required to audit and report on undergraduate classes, to watch the curriculum in action, and to undertake assignments in writing, performing, and listening from the standpoint of the teacher. Lectures on L & M, from a number of points of view, are given by President Schuman and members of the L & M faculty. The appearance of this report now makes generally available much of the material that has developed in this course and that has, in some degree, formed its content.

APPENDIX 1

Details of Organization of
L & M Curriculum

A. FLEXIBILITY OF PROGRAM

As ORIGINALLY planned, the curriculum in Literature and Materials was divided into year-by-year classes: L & M I, L & M II, L & M III, and L & M IV. L & M I and II were considered as years of general study and background; L & M III and IV were considered as years of specialization, the students being divided into special sections for pianists, singers, composers, orchestral instrumentalists. L & M V was devoted to a summarizing course in Music History. Supplementary courses were offered in Orchestration, Orchestral Conducting, and other subjects.

It was felt that the objectives of the curriculum could be more consistently attained by the plan now in operation. Ideally, one of the school's objectives has been the inclusion of all non-performance skills (i.e., those aspects of study not specifically in the province of the major teacher, orchestral conductor, choral director, or chamber music instructor) directly in the L & M class work. Thus orchestration, for example, is considered not as a separate branch of study, but as a technique to be examined in the context of music studied as a whole.

The L & M teacher is evidently given a far greater burden of responsibility under the new plan. He cannot "pass" a borderline student on to another class and another instructor. He will have the student as long as the student is in school, and must eventually decide on a just disposition of the case.

The flexibility of the present organization of L & M offers untold advantages, while at the same time it requires much good will and ingenuity on the part of the faculty to realize these advantages. It is possible for L & M instructors to "exchange" students for longer or shorter periods, in order to pursue special studies or to become acquainted with other viewpoints or approaches. The L & M teacher may consult with the student's major teacher, with the L & M Planning Committee, with the Dean, or with other faculty members regarding special problems of the student, and may devise special courses of study as a result.

B. SCHEDULE AND TEACHING LOAD

The fifteen hours weekly devoted to L & M are utilized by the instructor entirely at his own discretion. Each student is expected to spend eight of these hours per week in L & M study. The instructor may require four two-hour classes, or six hours of class plus two hours of private conference, or he may divide the time in any other way that seems most effective. The full-time L & M "teaching load" is the fifteen hours per week, through which the L & M activities may be spread. (At present, the fifteen hours are

consecutive, from Tuesday noon through 2.30 p.m. on
Thursday. This plan leaves Monday and Friday clear for
academic classes, rehearsals, and other activities of the
School, and facilitates the planning of schedules by all instructors.)

C. TEACHING FELLOWS

The L & M instructor is assisted in handling his group
of students by one or two Teaching Fellows. The Teaching Fellowship program is an integral part of L & M and
is intended to provide a small number of gifted and interested graduates with an opportunity to pursue further
studies while gaining actual apprenticeship experience in
teaching. Candidates are selected each year on the basis
of undergraduate records and probable aptitude as future
teachers. The Fellowships carry tuition scholarships and
small stipends. Each Fellow is assigned to work with one
of the members of the L & M faculty. The first duty of
the Fellow is to observe; the second is to assist the teacher
in such ways as the latter considers practical, on the basis
of the Fellow's ability and experience. Teaching Fellows
are often entrusted with the day-to-day conduct of beginning classes in ear-training, sight-singing, fundamentals of music, or secondary instruction in piano. They
work, however, in all cases under the supervision of the
instructor to whom they are assigned. Although the Fellow is, in a sense, a teacher-in-training, it is emphasized
that the L & M instructor is to work *with* the Fellow
rather than have the Fellow work *for* him.

Teaching Fellowships in L & M are renewable, and
most have been held for two-year periods. A Fellow in

his second year, having had considerable experience, is usually able to give real assistance to the instructor. It is often possible for the instructor to arrange to have two classes or sections in operation simultaneously: one conducted by himself and the other under the supervision of an experienced Fellow. Each L & M instructor has, at all times, two rooms at his disposition for precisely such cases.

D. POINTS

Since the student spends eight hours per week in L & M, and since L & M covers all aspects of work in music theory, the student receives eight points credit per semester, or a total of sixty-four for a normal four-year course of study. (This credit has been approved by the State of New York in so far as it concerns the granting of the Bachelor of Science Degree in Music.)

E. GRADES

Since the student no longer "passes" from class to class, grades in L & M assume a meaning somewhat different from the usual. In any curriculum involving year-by-year courses, it is possible for the student with minimum passing grades to progress as rapidly as the student with a straight "A" average. The L & M curriculum requires a different sort of expression of satisfactory or unsatisfactory work and progress. The student file, or "dossier" (see Appendix 2) in actuality is a comprehensive and continuous report on work. But since some manner of grading is still required, a uniform system was adopted at

Juilliard in 1952. This is explained in the following memorandum from the Dean of Juilliard School:

It has become increasingly clear during recent years that our present grading system contains certain inequities which often lead to misunderstandings as to the precise meaning of these grades. Since the letters we now use (A, B, C, etc.) do not have specific adjectives attached to them, there has been no unanimity in the conception of the meaning of these marks. In addition, there has been a lack of relationship between grading in the major study and in the class subjects.

In order to overcome these and other difficulties connected with grading, we are instituting, effective immediately, an entirely new system. We have found that the most equitable grading for use at the School was that employed at entrance examinations where, rather than asking the faculty to assign an abstract letter, various adjectives were used. We believe—and the New York State Department of Higher Education concurs—that by making a similar arrangement in all grading we will achieve the desired uniformity.

There follows a list of grades and abbreviations for those grades which we will use in the future:

> E—Exceptional, Outstanding;
> S—Superior;
> G—Good, Average;
> P—Passing, Adequate;
> W—Weak, Barely Passing, Probation;
> F—Failing.

F.   L & M PLANNING COMMITTEE

Matters of policy, details of day-to-day operation, and all problems not on the top administrative level of the School are handled by the Planning Committee of the L & M faculty, which functions in lieu of a Chairman or Head of Department. This committee is appointed by the President and consists of the Assistant Dean, *ex officio*, the Secretary of the L & M faculty, and three members of the faculty. The Planning Committee meets weekly, and there are occasional meetings throughout the year of the entire L & M faculty.

Note: As has been stated in President Schuman's Introduction, the L & M Planning Committee has been replaced by a departmental Chairman. The Planning Committee, however, was a functioning body during the years covered by this report.

APPENDIX 2

———◆•◆———

Student "Dossier," Filled Out as a Sample

THE following pages represent thirteen pages of a student's "dossier," the use and purpose of which is explained in Part III.

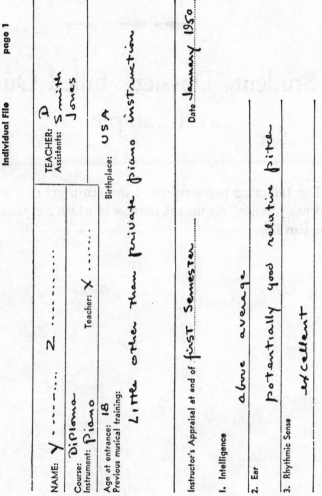

Individual File   page 1

NAME: Y........ Z ....

TEACHER: D
Assistants: Smith
           Jones

Course: Diploma
Instrument: Piano   Teacher: X ....

Age at entrance: 18
Previous musical training: Birthplace: USA

Little other than private piano instruction

Instructor's Appraisal at end of First Semester.........   Date January 1950

1. Intelligence   above average

2. Ear   potentially good relative pitch

3. Rhythmic Sense   excellent

178

4. Co-ordination

good

5. Musical background (Information, experience)

very little

6. General Cultural Background

Highschool, Radio, TV

7. Diligence

good

8. Miscellaneous comment

An interested and interesting student. Has responded extremely well to first taste of intensive musical Training. Some problems of adjustment to atmosphere of big city. Is inclined to become overly competitive.

BASIC MATERIALS
RUDIMENTS OF MUSIC

If student is qualified on entrance, check here ☐

	Work Assigned	Completion
SCALES { eye ear	OK	
MODES { eye ear	Study and discussion of early music in class	Feb. 1951
SIGNATURES	OK	
CLEFS Treble Alto Tenor Bass	Chorales in open Score (Riemenschneider)	Spring 1950
INTERVALS (Aural & Visual recognition)	Special Classes in ear Training	Spring 1950

PITCH DISCRIMINATION*	Easy Sonatas with String Players	Still has difficulty
RHYTHM, METRE, PULSE	OK	
RECOGNITION OF INSTRUMENTS	attendance at orchestra rehearsals	Spring 1950
OTHERS		

*Should include tests on whether:
  a) steady or wavering
  b) sharp or flat

Student passed Basic Vocabulary Test

Date: Feb 1951

Grade: 92 %

WORKS STUDIED INTENSIVELY

Composer	Work	Manner of Study*	Date
A. [Up to 16th Century] include Machault, Josquin, Plain Chant, Organum	Gregorian Chant, Machault - Mass, Josquin - examples, H A M	lecture, class performance, lecture, recording; Study of rhythm + metre	'49-'50, 50-'5, 52-53
B. [16th Century] Palestrina, Lassus	Palestrina} motets Lassus, Byrd - madrigals, Palestrina Motets	lecture, class performance; melodic analysis used as models 16th cent. counterpoint	49-50, 50-51
C. [1600-1750] Gabrieli, Monteverde, Schuetz, Purcell, Lully, Rameau, Couperin, Scarlatti, Bach, Handel	Handel - Trio Sonata, Bach - chorals, - 2 part inventions, Purcell - 3 part fantasies, Bach - WTC, I:4/II:12, Gabrieli-Canzone, septim toni, Bach - Magnificat, Rameau, Lully, Cesti...	performance, harmonic analysis; analysis; performance and analysis; lecture, analysis; lecture and performance, analysis, formal + melodic; class paper on 18th cent. French figure 52-53	49-50, 50-51, 51-52

	Composers / Works	Method	Dates
D. (Classical Period) Haydn, Mozart, Beethoven, Gluck	Haydn – Piano Sonata in C, String Quartet Gluck – Dimunités du Styx Beethoven – Symphony I { Piano Sonata op.2 III Mozart – " " in F Beethoven – op.53 II, op.95 Mozart – 2nd act finale, Figaro	harmonic and structural analysis lecture, melodic analysis harmonic, formal analysis lecture and analysis	49-50 50-51 51-52 52-53
E. (19th Century) Schubert, Schumann, Chopin, Wagner, Liszt, Franck, Verdi, Moussorgsky, Brahms	Brahms – Alto Rhapsody Schumann – Kinderszenen Schubert – 3 Songs Wagner – Tristan, overture Chopin – F major Ballad Schubert – C major Symph. last mvmt Schumann – Karneval	class performance and elementary analysis harmonic analysis " formal and harmonic analysis performance	49-50 50-51 51-52 52-53
F. (20th Century) Debussy, Fauré, Ravel, Stravinsky, Bartok, Hindemith, Schoenberg, Les Six, Americans	Fauré, Debussy – Songs Hindemith – Ludus tonalis No 4 Copland – outdoor Overture Stravinsky – MASS Debussy – 2 Preludes Bartok – Violin Sonata, II Schoenberg – op.11, 19, 23 Schuman – Judith	harmonic analysis lecture and analysis lecture " " harmonic analysis analysis harmonic performance formal and harmonic analysis	50-51 51-52 52-53

Note: Names of composers are listed merely as reminders of essential material.

*May include: Lecture, class performance, homework analysis, etc.

ENSEMBLE WORKS PERFORMED

Work	Date performed	Comment
Mozart - Trio B♭	Nov. '49	Competent technically. Does not seem to listen to himself or partner. Little understanding of style.
Beethoven - Violin Sonata a minor	Feb. '50	Surprisingly good in livery way
Copland Violin Sonata	Dec. '50	Very romantic approach. (rubato in slow movement, "beautiful" finale.) Senses hopelessness in this music, but blames it on composer. Complains of "unpianistic sounds."

Work	Date	Comments
Beethoven - Vln Sonata in C minor	March '51	Well prepared, pianistically. Ensemble problems not realized. Balance generally poor. Slow movement not worked out.
Mozart - 2 Piano Sonata in D	Jan. '52	Excellent performance. Recommended for Wednesday Series.
Bartok - Sonata for 2 pianos and percussion	April '52	Not yet on performance level, but intentions are good. First movement seems too difficult at this time.
Harris - Quintet	Dec. '52	Very good, indeed. Straightforward performance. Good ensemble.
Brahms - Trio in C minor	March '53	Played as "dress" for Friday night performance. Suggested slower tempo for 1st movement. Should be good.

WRITING SKILLS

A. Counterpoint

	2-part	3-part
I. Cantus Firmus (including Species Counterpoint)	Review October '51. Passed	Showed no difficulty in this area. Passed comprehensive Class Test March '51
II. Free Counterpoint	No trouble with the "rules", but work in this area is more difficult for him than C.F. Passed March '51	Motets in the style of Palestrina good. Dec. '51 Piece for String Trio fair Jan. '52

III. Imitative Counterpoint
Canon
pre-fugal types
Fugue

Canon Nov. 51	2 fugue expositions
Inventions and one	March, April '52
fugue exposition March '52	Fugue for Piano (not
	written for class)
Review october 52	Performed Jan. '53
	competent.

Note I: Stylistic range of assignments and studies:
   All the above should be considered through the changes in style of various periods.

Note II: Instructor will fill in *date* and *estimate* of work, merely as a check. (For example: 2-part canon, 1953, satisfactory.) Examples of work are to be attached to student's file.

WRITING SKILLS

B. Harmony

(Check work completed and make comment, if necessary, on additional page.)

*1. TRADITIONAL HARMONY (1700-1900)

elementary _ok_
advanced

- ✓ a. chorale harmonization
- ✓ b. harmonization (free) of melody
- ✓ c. construction of harmonic phrase
- ✓ d. ground bass
- ✓ e. figured bass (17th, 18th centuries)
- ✓ f. modulation (theory & technique)
- ✓ g. compositional techniques
- ✓ h. harmonic forms: dance forms to sonata
-   i. stylistic differentiation in traditional harmony

2. "NON-TRADITIONAL" HARMONY

- ✓ a. pre-tonal "harmony"
- ✓ b. evolution of tonality

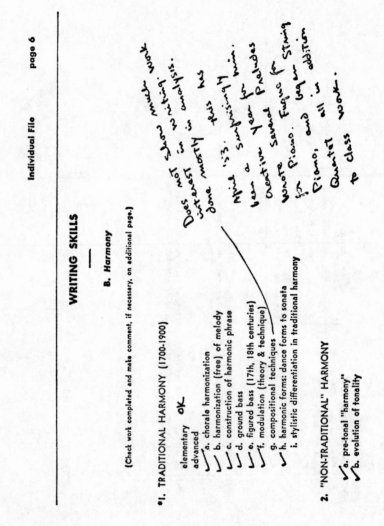

Does not show much work
interest in writing. Analysis.
done mostly this has

April '53. Surprising him.
Been a year for his
Creation several Preludes
where Piano. Fugue for String
for Piano, and organ
Quartet all in addition
to class work.

✓c. dissolution of tonality
✓d. contemporary harmonic techniques

* HARMONIC TECHNIQUES OF:
  1. Corelli — A. Scarlatti
  2. Bach — Handel
  3. Mozart
  4. Beethoven
  5. Weber — Schumann — Mendelssohn
  6. Wagner
  7. Chopin
  8. Brahms
  9. Franck
  10. R. Strauss — Mahler — Reger

WRITING SKILLS

C. Melody Writing

(Check work completed and make comment, if necessary, on additional page.)

I. MODAL

✓ a. with text } Analysis and written work
✓ b. without text

TONAL

✓ a. with text } analysis OK, written work not very
✓ b. without text   apt, but competent by
✓ c. In idiomatic instrumental terms   way of illustration

ATONAL

✓ a. with text } Showed some interest in 12-tone
✓ b. without text   technique. Suspect as an escape
✓ c. in idiomatic instrumental terms   into "rules" rather than as a creative
                                            idiom.

✓ II. ORNAMENTATION OR ELABORATION OF MELODY

✓ III. ELEMENTARY MELODIC VARIATION ?

D. Notation

✓ I. NEATNESS AND LEGIBILITY yes; but it was a struggle.

✓ II. CORRECT USE OF ORTHOGRAPHIC CONVENTIONS
generally, yes.

✓ III. CORRECT EDITING OF MS.

    a. phrase
    b. syllable
    c. other

when he tries or is made to try.

LISTENING SKILLS

(Check work completed and make comment, if necessary, on additional page.)

I. STEPS BEYOND "BASIC VOCABULARY":

✓ 1. Dictation
    ✓ a. Melody   OK
    ✓ b. Simple Harmony more difficulty here than in other areas.
    c. 2-part writing OK

✓ 2. Tonal Memory (Simple units: melody, harmony, etc.)

✓ 3. Recognition of more complex musical units

II. ABILITY TO RECOGNIZE COMPOSITIONAL DEVICES:

✓ 1. To recognize and discuss what happens to a theme or motif
    a. transposition
    b. fragmentation
    c. inversion, augmentation, etc.
    d. extension, etc., etc.

2. To perceive structural unity of a given composition, not only in terms of conventional "formal" analysis, but much more in terms of internal logic and meaning. *Can follow a rule, but has more difficulty in applying a principle. Must learn to listen.*

3. To be aware of the functions of musical material at various points of development in a composition.

III. ABILITY TO RECOGNIZE BROAD STYLE DIVISONS, AND TO SHOW SOME UNDERSTANDING OF THE PROGRESS OF STYLISTIC CHANGE IN THE HISTORY AND DEVELOPMENT OF WESTERN MUSIC.

IV. RELATION OF ABOVE TO PERFORMANCE, IN TERMS OF CRITICISM.

Tends to think in theoretical Terms.

Thus, there is often a) no real application of underlying musical principles

b) tenacious defense on theoretical grounds of mannerisms which have no relation to performance. Must learn to listen.

PERFORMING SKILLS

A. Primary

(at student's major instrument)

	Works Performed	Date	Proficiency
Sight-Reading	Mozart - 2 piano Sonata in F	1949	only fair
	Schumann - Pictures from the East (2 piano)	1949	poor
	Mozart, Haydn - Violin Sonatas, Trios	'50-'51	fair
	Accompanied Songs (Schubert, Schumann Fauré)	'52	in moving
	Brahms Quintet in f (Student who prepared it absent)	'52	Surprisingly good, but on exam proficient
Keyboard Harmony (for Pianists)		Passed April 1951	
Ensemble	See page 4		

B. Secondary

Sight-Singing	Assigned to Special Classes qualified	April 1952.	Competant in general. Greatest weakness: Intonation
Keyboard (for non-pianists)			
Conducting	Rudiments Preparation of Madrigals	March '51 Jan. Feb '52	OK very good
Score-Reading	Coached Bartok - 2 piano Sonata Exercises from Morris-Ferguson Bach chorales, Riemenschneider Haydn String Quartets Str. Q. Haydn, Beethoven op. 18, I	April '52 2nd Sem. '49-50 Nov. 50 Jan. 51 1952	on the whole, good OK OK fair fair
Others	Orchestration - Scored 2 Bach choral Preludes	1952	OK

195

READING ASSIGNMENTS

Author	Work	Date Assigned	Comment
Copland, Aaron	What to Listen for in Music	'49 - '50	
Hindemith, Paul	Traditional Harmony		
Piston, Walter	Counterpoint	'50 - '51	
Hindemith, Paul	the Craft of Musical Composition		
Eschmann, Karl	Changing Forms in Modern Music	'51 - '52	
Leibowitz, René	Schoenberg and His School		

Piston, Walter — Harmony

Salzer, Felix — Structural Hearing '52 -'53

Sessions, Roger — the Musical Experience

Copland, Aaron — Music and Imagination

Smith, Cecil — worlds of Music

SPECIAL ASSIGNMENTS — REPORTS — ACTIVITIES

Date	Assignment or Activity	Comment
'49 - '50	Member of Trio in class	Prepared a Mozart Trio for class performance and discussion. Read written class assignments for this combination of instruments. After Transfer of 'cellist to another class section, he continued with violinist. Performed several Sonatas in class.
Jan. '50 - spring '51	Member of Violin + Piano Team	

Fall '51	Member of Two Piano Team	Performed 2 works for this combination. Sight read 2 piano arrangements of orchestral scores for class sessions in conducting.
Jan. '52	Preparation and class performances of motets and madrigals	Competent, but tends to lose himself in details.
'52 - '53	Paper on harmonic structure of the second act Finale of Mozart's "Figaro". Paper on 18th century French piano writing.	Extensive research. An interesting and in some ways quite original treatment of subject. Included self-made records to illustrate points.

199

ASSIGNMENTS TO SPECIAL CLASSES

Including Piano Repertoire
Vocal Repertoire
Special Ear-Training
Special Keyboard

Date	Class	Comment
1949-51	Keyboard	Not assigned to special class. Work completed in regular class. April '51
1949-56	Ear-Training	Serious Student. Needs elementary Training but is making good progress.

1950-51	Ear Training	Sight-singing improved; some difficulties with pitch. Melodic dictation: good. Harmonic dictation: a little slow but accurate.
1951-'52	Piano repertoire	Very good student. However, suspect he prefers talking about music to applying his knowledge in practical terms. Passed: April 1952
'52-'53	Ear training / Piano repertoire	A good year. Has performed in class on several occasions. Special interest in 18th Century.

NOTE: Instructors of Special Classes will give the major L & M *instructor* a brief report on student's work. It is the major L & M instructor's responsibility to see that records are attached to this file.

GENERAL NOTES ON STUDENT'S ATTITUDE, PROGRESS, ETC.

A serious, talented and intelligent boy.
While never a problem in class, he has, at times,
been a problem to himself.   He is inclined to
cling to half-formed conclusions based on largely
theoretical considerations to the detriment of
his practical objectives. As an example, I might
mention his distaste, in his earlier years at
School, for any music between Bach and
Beethoven.   He managed to compound this
dislike by constant efforts to "prove" his
point in mutual arguments, in the preparation
of which he must have gone to considerable

Trouble. Paradoxically enough, he spent his last year on two major projects (of his own choosing), in the course of which he demonstrated not only real insight into the music of the eighteenth century, but honest love and understanding for the work of composers he has sought to reject.

APPENDIX 3

---◆---

Programs of L & M Concerts

A—WEDNESDAY ONE O'CLOCK CONCERT SERIES

The Wednesday One O'Clock Concert Series is designed to supplement the class work in Literature and Materials of Music I and II. Students and faculty perform in these concerts, which are attended only by students and faculty members of the School.

OCTOBER 25, 1950

Henry Purcell—*Altisidora's song, "From Rosy Bowers,"* from the opera Don Quixote (1695)
(Five Stages of Madness of a Lady Distraught by Love: Sullenly Mad. Mirthfully Mad—a swift movement. Melancholy Madness. Fantastically Mad. Stark Mad.)

Henry Purcell—*Bonduca's Air, from the opera Bonduca* (1695)

Claude Debussy—*Syrinx* (1912)

Joseph Haydn—*String Quartet, "Sunrise," Op. 76, No. 4, in B flat* (1797)

NOVEMBER 1, 1950

Organ Music of the Renaissance Period
1. Hofhaymer (1459–1537)—*On Freudt Verzer*
2. Titelouze (1563–1633)—*Pange Lingua*
3. de Cabezon (1510–1566)—*Diferencias Sobre el Canto del Caballero*

Joseph Haydn—*Sonata in A flat* (1785)
Jean-Louis Martinet—*Prelude and Fugue, in C, for two pianos* (1942) (First American Performance)

NOVEMBER 8, 1950

Henry Cowell—*Suite for Woodwinds* (1933)
George Friedrich Handel—*Trio Sonata in E flat* (ca. 1720)
Johann Sebastian Bach—*Partita No. 2, in D minor* (ca. 1720) *for unaccompanied violin*

NOVEMBER 15, 1950—The Juilliard Orchestra

Gioacchino Rossini—*"L'Italiana in Algeri"—Overture* (1813)
Joseph Haydn—*Symphony in D Minor* (1784—published for the first time in 1937)
Aaron Copland—*"Billy the Kid"—Ballet Suite* (1941)

NOVEMBER 22, 1950

Serge Prokofiev—*Sonata in D, No. 1, for violin and piano* (1946)
Johannes Brahms—*Capriccio in F-sharp minor, Op. 76, No. 1* (1878)
—*Ballade in G minor, Op. 118, No. 3* (1892)
—*Intermezzo in E-flat minor, Op. 118, No. 6* (1892)
—*Capriccio in C major, Op. 76, No. 8* (1878)

Samuel Scheidt—*"Sinfonie"* (1650)

NOVEMBER 29, 1950

Gabriel Fauré—*Clair de Lune* (1887)
—*Au Cimitière* (1889)
—*En Sourdine* (1890)
—*Automne* (1880)
—*Mai* (1865)
Claude Debussy—*Six Epigraphes Antiques* (1915)
Johannes Brahms—*Two songs for contralto, with viola and piano, Op. 91* (1863–1884)
  Gestillte Sehnsucht
  Geistliches Wiegenlied

DECEMBER 6, 1950

César Franck—*Prélude, Choral et Fugue* (1884)
Paul Hindemith—*Sonata for trombone and piano* (1942)
Gregorian Chants—sung by the Liturgical Choir of the Church of St. Francis de Sales, New York.

THE JUILLIARD CHORUS

William Billings (1751–1800)—*Modern Music*
Supply Belcher (1751–1836)—*Spring, "Set down that glass!" Invitation*
William Billings—*Retrospect (from "The Singing Master's Assistant,"* 1778)

DECEMBER 13, 1950—Juilliard Opera Theatre Seminar

A Studio Performance of *Gianni Schicchi;* Opera in One Act. *Libretto by* GIOVACCHINO FORZANO, *Music by* GIACOMO PUCCINI. (First performance: New York City, 1918). *English Translation by* PERCY PITT

JANUARY 10, 1951

Giuseppe Tartini—*Sonata for violin and piano, "Devil's Trill"* (1714)
Aaron Copland—*Sonata for piano* (1941)
Paul Hindemith—*Sonata for violin and piano in E* (1935)

JANUARY 17, 1951—The Juilliard Orchestra,
Section II

Samuel Barber—*Capricorn Concerto, Op. 21* (1944)
Erik Satie—*Five Very Little Dances, from the lyric comedy, "The Snare of Medusa"* (1921)
Ludwig van Beethoven—*Symphony No. 2 in D, Op. 36* (1802)

JANUARY 24, 1951—*Special Concert Demonstration of a Copy of Mozart's Piano*

Carl Philipp Emanuel Bach—*Sonata in F minor* (1781). From, "Essay on the True Art of Playing Keyboard Instruments."
Joseph Haydn—*Sonata in E flat, Op. 66* (1789)
Wolfgang Amadeus Mozart—*Sonata in A, K. 331* (1778)

JANUARY 31, 1951

Wolfgang Amadeus Mozart—*Sonata for Piano in F (four hands), K. 497* (1786)
Arnold Schoenberg—*Two Piano Pieces, Op. 33a, Op. 33b* (1932)
Charles Edward Ives—*Two Piano Pieces* (1908 and 1909)
   "Some Southpaw Pitching"
   "The Anti-abolitionist Riots of the 1830's and 1840's"
Wolfgang Amadeus Mozart—*Quintet in E flat for violin, two violas, horn, and cello, K. 407* (1783)

FEBRUARY 7, 1951

Giovanni Gabrieli—*Canzon Septimi Toni* (Mixolydian, transposed) (1597)
Giovanni Gabrieli—*Canzon Duodecimi Toni* (Hypo-Ionian, transposed) (1597)
Ludwig van Beethoven—*String Quartet, Op. 18, No. 3 in D* (1800)
Maurice Ravel—*"Miroirs"* (1905)

FEBRUARY 14, 1951—The Juilliard Orchestra, Section II

Luigi Boccherini—*Cello concerto in B flat* (ca. 1800)
Charles Edward Ives—*Symphony No. 3* (ca. 1905)
Ernest Chausson—*Poème, Op. 25, for violin and orchestra* (1896)

FEBRUARY 21, 1951

Franz Liszt—*Ballade, No. 2, in B minor* (1854)
Franz Schubert—*"Der Hirt Auf Dem Felsen"* (1828)
Francis Poulenc—*Air Grave* (1928); *Air Champetre* (1928)
Paul Hindemith—*Sonata for bassoon and piano* (1938)
Leonard Bernstein—*"I Hate Music"* (1943)

FEBRUARY 28, 1951

Ludwig van Beethoven—*Sonata for cello and piano in A, Op. 69* (1809)
Erik Satie—*Three Pieces in the Form of a Pear, for Two Pianos* (1903)
Wolfgang Amadeus Mozart—*Piano trio in E, K. 542* (1788)

March 7, 1951

Paul Hindemith—*Das Marienleben* (1948)

March 28, 1951

Heinrich Schütz—*Ich Danke Den Herrn von Ganzem Herzen* (1636) (*Kleine Geistliche Konzerte, Teil I, No. 3*)—Text: Psalm III
Was Hast Du Werwirket (1636) (*Kleine Geistliche Konzerte, Teil II, No. 2*)—Text from Meditations of St. Augustine
Franz Schubert—*Quartettsatz in C minor* (1820). From the unfinished quartet, No. 9
Robert Schumann—*Davidsbündlertänze* (1837)

April 4, 1951—The Juilliard Orchestra, Section II

Johann Sebastian Bach—*Suite for Orchestra, No. 4 in D* (1733)
Philippot—*Overture* (1949)
Wolfgang Amadeus Mozart—*Concerto for Two Pianos and Orchestra, in E flat, K. 365* (1779)

April 11, 1951

Ludwig van Beethoven—*Sonata No. 1, Opus 12, for Violin and Piano* (1798)
John Ireland—*The Land of Lost Content* (1921)
Igor Stravinsky—*Octet for Wind Instruments* (1922)

April 18, 1951

Béla Bartók—*Sonata No. 1, for Violin and Piano* (1921)
Walter Piston—*Divertimento for Nine Instruments* (1946)

APRIL 25, 1951—The Juilliard Orchestra,
Section II

Paul Hindemith—*Overture "Neues vom Tage"* (1929)
Ludwig van Beethoven—*Piano Concerto No. 3 in C minor, Op. 37* (1800)
Richard Strauss—*"Till Eulenspiegel's Merry Pranks," Op. 28* (1895)

MAY 2, 1951

Bohuslav Martinu—*Sonata No. 1, for Violin and Piano* (1930)
Gustav Mahler—*"Rheinlegendchen"* (1888)
—*"Ich Atmet' Einen Linden Duft"* (1902)
—*"Blicke Mir Nicht in Die Lieder"* (1902)
—*"Ich Bin Der Welt Abhanden Gekommen"* (1902)
—*"Ablosung Im Sommer"* (1888)
—*"Das Irdische Leben"* (1888)
Samuel Barber—*Sonata for Piano* (1949)

MAY 9, 1951

Johannes Brahms—*Sonata for Clarinet and Piano in E flat, Op. 120, No. 2* (1894)
Alban Berg—*Sonata No. 1, for Piano* (1908)
Virgil Thomson—*Sonata da Chiesa* (1926)

MAY 16, 1951—Program of Modern Dance
with Music by Student Composers

MAY 23, 1951—Special Concert of
Harpsichord Music

Giles Farnaby (ca. 1560–1600)—*Group of two pieces: His Rest, His Dream*

Jean Philippe Rameau (1683–1764)—*Deux Rigaudons: Musette Rondeau*
Antonio Soler (1729–1783)—*Two Sonatas*
Johann Sebastian Bach (1685–1750)—*Chromatic Fantasy and Fugue*
Domenico Scarlatti (1685–1757)—*Sonata in D, Sonata in G*

B—FRIDAY EVENING SERIES

NOVEMBER 3, 1950—The Juilliard Orchestra

Richard Wagner—*"The Flying Dutchman"—Overture* (1843)
Wolfgang Amadeus Mozart—*Symphony No. 39 in E-flat, K. 543* (1788)
Virgil Thomson—*"Wheat Field at Noon"* (1948)
David Diamond—*Symphony No. 3* (1945)

NOVEMBER 10, 1950—The Juilliard String Quartet

Giuseppe Verdi—*String Quartet in E Minor* (1873)
Ludwig van Beethoven—*String Quartet, Op. 59, No. 1* (1806)
Béla Bartók—*String Quartet No. 6* (1939)

DECEMBER 8, 1950—The Juilliard Orchestra

Béla Bartók—*Concerto for Orchestra* (1943)
Ernest Bloch—*Concertino for Flute, Viola and Orchestra* (1950). First performance, commissioned by the Juilliard Musical Foundation
César Franck—*Symphony in D minor* (1886–1888)

DECEMBER 15, 1950—A Concert of Chamber Music

Wolfgang Amadeus Mozart—*Quartet in D for Flute and Strings, K. 285* (1777)

Ben Weber—*Concerto for Piano Solo, Cello and Winds, Op. 32* (1950)
Darius Milhaud—*Sonata for Flute, Oboe, Clarinet and Piano* (1918)
Ludwig van Beethoven—*Trio for Piano, Violin and Cello, in E-flat, Op. 1, No. 1* (1795)

DECEMBER 18, 1950—A Special Concert of the Chamber Music of Alban Berg, presented for the benefit of the Student Aid Fund

Seven Songs of Youth (1905–1907)
Four pieces for Clarinet and Piano, Op. 5 (1913)
Piano Sonata, Op. 1 (1908)
Two Songs (Unedited—Extract from "Die Musik" 1930). (First performance)
  1. "Schliesse mir die augen beide . . ." (Tonal version, 1900)
  2. "Schliesse mir die augen beide . . ." (Twelve-tone version, 1926)
Four Songs, Op. 2 (1908–1909)
  1. From "Dem Schmerz sein Recht" (Hebbel)
2–4. Three Songs from "Der Glühende" (Mombert)
Lyric Suite (1925–1926)

JANUARY 12, 1951—Forty-sixth Anniversary Concert in honor of the founding of the Institute of Musical Art, January 16, 1905—The Juilliard String Quartet

Wolfgang Amadeus Mozart—*Quartet in A Major, K. 464* (1785)
William Bergsma—*Second String Quartet* (1944)

Franz Schubert—*Quartet in D Minor, No. 14* (Posthumous) ("Death and the Maiden")

JANUARY 19, 1951—A Concert of Chamber Music

Franz Danzi—*Quintet in E minor, Op. 67, No. 2* (ca. 1800)
Vincent Persichetti—*Pastoral for Quintet of Wind Instruments* (1943)
Roger Goeb—*Quintet for Woodwinds* (1949)
Gabriel Fauré—*Piano Quartet No. 1, in C minor, Op. 15* (1879)

JANUARY 26, 1951—The Juilliard Orchestra

Ludwig van Beethoven—*"Egmont" Overture, Op. 84* (1810)
Richard Strauss—*"Don Quixote," Op. 35* (1897)
Claude Debussy—*"La Mer," Three Symphonic Sketches* (1903–1904)

FEBRUARY 2, 1951—A Concert of Chamber Music

Joseph Haydn—*String Quartet in G minor, Op. 74, No. 3, "The Rider"* (1793)
Maurice Ravel—*Introduction and Allegro for Harp, String Quartet, Flute and Clarinet* (1905–1906)
Igor Stravinsky—*L'Histoire du Soldat* (1918)

FEBRUARY 16, 1951—Memorial Concert for Dr. Frank
        Damrosch (1859–1937)—The Juilliard
        Chorus and the Juilliard Orchestra

William Billings—*"Modern Music," from "The Psalm-Singer's Amusement"* (1781)

Robert Parris—"*The Hollow Men*" (T. S. Eliot) (1949)
(First Performance)
Robert Starer—*Five Proverbs on Love* (1950)
Irving Fine—"*The Hour Glass*" (1950) (Ben Jonson)
William Billings—"*Retrospect.*" An anthem of the
American Revolution, from the "Singing Master's As-
sistant" (1778)
Claude Debussy—"*The Blessed Damozel*" (1888)

FEBRUARY 23, 1951—The Juilliard String Quartet

Joseph Haydn—*String Quartet in F, Op. 77* (1799)
William Schuman—*String Quartet No. 4* (1950)
Ludwig van Beethoven—*String Quartet in F, Op. 135,
No. 16* (1826)

MARCH 2, 1951—A Concert of Chamber Music

Franz Schubert—*Piano Trio in E flat, Op. 100* (1827)
Mark Schubart—"*Yvan to Claire*": *Four Love Songs for
soprano and strings* (1948)
Walter Piston—*Sonata for Flute and Piano* (1930)
Paul Hindemith—*Septet for Wind Instruments* (1948)
(First New York Performance)

MARCH 15, 16, 17, 19, 1951—The Juilliard Opera
Theatre

The Prisoner, A Prologue and One Act, *by* LUIGI DALLA-
PICCOLA—First Performances in America

Text after "La torture par l'espérance" by Conte Villiers
de L'Isle-Adam and "The Legend of Ulenspiegel and
Lamme Goedzak" by Charles de Coster. English translation by Harold Heiberg, commissioned by the School for
the Juilliard Opera Theatre. New orchestral version by

Luigi Dallapiccola, commissioned by the School for the Juilliard Opera Theatre.

MARCH 30, 1951—A Concert of Chamber Music

Johann Sebastian Bach—*Overture in the French Style (B minor Partita)* (1735)
Johannes Brahms—*Sonata No. 2, in F, for Cello and Piano, Op. 99* (1885)
Bernard Wagenaar—*String Quartet No. 2* (1931)

APRIL 6, 1951—Concert in Memory of
Ernest Hutcheson (1871–1951)

Johann Sebastian Bach—*Prelude*—"*Gottes Zeit ist die allerbeste Zeit*" (1707)
Johann Sebastian Bach—*Chromatic Fantasy and Fugue* (1730)
Wolfgang Amadeus Mozart—*Motet, "Exsultate, jubilate," K. 165* (1730)
Frederic Chopin—*Sonata No. 2, in B flat minor, Op. 35* (1836)

APRIL 13, 1951—A Concert of Chamber Music

Ludwig van Beethoven—*Quintet for Piano and Winds in E flat, Op. 16* (1797)
Maurice Ravel—*Histoires Naturelles* (1906). Text by Jules Renard
Wolfgang Amadeus Mozart—*Sonata for Two Pianos in D, K. 448* (1781)
Roy Harris—*Trio for Piano, Violin and Cello* (1934)

APRIL 24, 1951—The Juilliard Orchestra

Igor Stravinsky—*Suite from "Pulcinella,"* (1919, revised 1949)

Samuel Barber—*Second Symphony* (1944)
Johannes Brahms—*Piano Concerto No. 2, in B flat, Op. 83* (1881)

APRIL 27, 1951—A Program of Choral Music
and Vocal Chamber Music. The
Juilliard Chorus and Soloists

William Schuman—*Prelude for Voices* (1939)
William Bergsma—*Let True Love Among Us Be* (1950)
Elliott Carter—*Musicians Wrestle Everywhere* (1945)
Dr. Thomas Arne—*Two Cantatas: 1. Delia; 2. The Morning* (ca. 1770)
Johannes Brahms—*Neue Liebeslieder Waltzer, Op. 65* (1877)
Maurice Ravel—*Trois Chansons* (1916)
Samuel Barber—*Dover Beach* (1936)
Johann Sebastian Bach—*Motet for Double Chorus: "Der Geist hilft unsrer Schwachheit auf"* (ca. 1720)

MAY 18, 1951—The Juilliard Orchestra

Nicolas Rimsky-Korsakoff—*Suite from the Opera "Tsar Saltan"* (1900)
Béla Bartók—*Concerto No. 3, for Piano and Orchestra* (1945)
Peter Mennin—*Symphony No. 5* (1950)

APPENDIX 4

———— ◆ ————

A Sample Comprehensive Examination in L & M (Sample Examination for Pianist)

PART A—EXAMINATION OF RECORD

I. The dossier shows that student entered in 1949, passed L & M I, II, III, grades of G and S.

II. In fourth year, instructor's appraisal showed above-average intelligence etc., but some weakness in ear-training. Dossier shows student did review drill sessions with instructor and showed satisfactory improvement. *Jury will check.*

III. File shows good general coverage of works and periods. Special fourth-year projects included:
Comparison of Bach and Mozart C Major fugues
Comparison of Mozart, Franck, Brahms, Copland variations

IV. Written examples of counterpoint show some

weaknesses. *Jury will check.* Very good in harmony. Original melodies show musicality. Notation neat and satisfactory.

V. Record on listening skills not conclusive. *Jury will check.*

VI. Jury will check sight-reading.

VII. Student completed Piano Repertoire I and II, grades of S.

PART B—ORAL

I. Jury checks all points noted above.

   1. *Ear:* Identify minor sixth, perfect fourth, major second, diminished fifth.

      Identify progression II, V, I.

      Repeat simple 10-note melody, played twice.

   2. *Counterpoint:* Student given five minutes to write a fourth-species counterpoint on nine-note cantus (three voices, two voices given).

      Student asked to comment on (or "correct") an example of contrapuntal writing (exercise). Student asked to give quick analysis of a short contrapuntal piece by Hindemith or other contemporary.

   3. *Listening skills:* Play an unfamiliar piece for student. Jury will pose questions:

      (*a*) composer or period?

      (*b*) form?

       (*c*) instruments?

       (*d*) harmonic or contra-
           puntal features?

       (*e*) *Sing* some portion of
           piece.

4. *Sight-reading:* Jury will check in usual fashion.

II. Free questioning by Jury. (Jury will bear in mind that student is a pianist.)

1. Jury will ask questions on piece just sight-read and may expand to include period, style, and study problems.

2. Jury will ask questions on knowledge of repertoire.

   Program building: Student may be given incomplete recital program consisting of large Schubert Sonata and group of Chopin Etudes.

      Problem: Complete program for afternoon recital at University of ———.

3. Discuss student's "favorite" string quartet. Check student's familiarity with this work, and with other *non-piano* repertoire.

4. Give brief harmonic outline of Exposition and Recapitulation of sonata played for graduation examination.

APPENDIX 5

Faculty of Juilliard School of Music

Mark Schubart, DEAN
Frederick Prausnitz, ASSISTANT DEAN

ORCHESTRAL CONDUCTING

Jean Morel (Conductor, The Juilliard Orchestra)

Frederick Prausnitz
Frederic Waldman

CHORAL CONDUCTING

Robert Hufstader
Ralph Hunter

Margaret Hillis (Assistant)

PIANO

Katherine Bacon
Joseph Bloch
Lonny Epstein
Irwin Freundlich
James Friskin
Sascha Gorodnitzki
Alton Jones
William Kapell

Rosina Lhevinne
Frances Mann
Josef Raieff
Gordon Stanley
Edward Steuermann
Rosalyn Tureck
Beveridge Webster

VOICE

Catherine Aspinall
Lucia Dunham

Evan Evans
Marion Szekely-Freschl

VOICE

Mack Harrell
Sergius Kagen
Florence Page Kimball
Edith Piper

Belle Julie Soudant
Dolf Swing
Bernard Taylor

STRINGED INSTRUMENTS

Dorothy de Lay (Violin)
Edouard Dethier (Violin)
Joseph Fuchs (Violin)
Ivan Galamian (Violin)
Bernard Greenhouse ('Cello)
Conrad Held (Violin and Viola)

Milton Katims (Viola)
Hans Letz (Violin and Viola)
Ronald Murat (Violin)
Louis Persinger (Violin)
Leonard Rose ('Cello)
Oscar Shumsky (Violin)
Luigi Silva ('Cello)

HARP

Marcel Grandjany

HARPSICHORD

Fernando Valenti

ORGAN

Lillian Carpenter
Bronson Ragan

Vernon de Tar

ORCHESTRAL INSTRUMENTS
Woodwind

Vincent Abato (Bass Clarinet and Saxophone)
Daniel Bonade (Clarinet)
Arthur Christmann (Clarinet)
Augustin Duquès (Clarinet)
Harold Gomberg (Oboe)

Simon Kovar (Bassoon)
Arthur Lora (Flute)
William Polisi (Bassoon)
Lois Wann (Oboe)
Frederick Wilkins (Flute)

Brass

William Bell (Tuba)
James Chambers (Horn)
Robert Schulze (Horn)
Davis Shuman (Trombone)
James Smith (Trumpet)

Roger Smith (Trombone)
Edward Treutel (Trumpet)
William Vacchiano (Trumpet)

Timpani and Percussion

Morris Goldenberg

Saul Goodman

Double Bass

Joseph De Angelis
Anselme Fortier
Stuart Sankey

John Schaeffer
Frederick Zimmermann

OPERA THEATRE

Frederic Cohen (Director)
Frederic Waldman (Associate Director and Conductor)
Frederick Kiesler (Scenic director)
Alberto Bimboni (Musical assistant)
Leo van Witsen (Stage makeup and costumes)

Ethelyn Dryden (Musical assistant)
Elsa Kahl (Musical acting)
Madeleine Marshall (Diction)
Viola Peters (Musical assistant)
Morton Siegel (Assistant Stage Director)

CHAMBER MUSIC AND ENSEMBLE

Edouard Dethier
Joseph Fuchs
Richard Franko Goldman
Marcel Grandjany
Frederic Hart
Raphael Hillyer *
Robert Hufstader

Robert Koff *
Hans Letz
Robert Mann *
Louis Persinger
Frederick Prausnitz
Beveridge Webster
Arthur Winograd *

COMPOSITION

William Bergsma
Vittorio Giannini
Peter Mennin

Vincent Persichetti
Bernard Wagenaar

LITERATURE AND MATERIALS OF MUSIC

William Bergsma
Joseph Bloch
Suzanne Bloch
Henry Brant
Jack Cox (Assistant)
Arnold Fish (Assistant)
Irwin Freundlich
Vittorio Giannini
Richard Franko Goldman (Chairman)
Frances Goldstein
Gordon Hardy (Assistant)

Frederic Hart
Mary Johnson
Sergius Kagen
Stoddard Lincoln (Assistant)
Norman Lloyd
Peter Mennin
Margaret Modlish (Assistant)
Vincent Persichetti
Robert Starer
Bernard Wagenaar
Robert Ward
Robert Witt (Assistant)

* Member, Juilliard String Quartet.

MUSICOLOGY

Robert Tangeman

ACADEMIC STUDIES

C. Harold Gray (Chairman)
Anne H. Berger (Education)
  (German)
George Makepeace (English)
Bernard Stambler (English)

Harry L. Robin (Acoustics)
Blanche Shattuck (History)
Norman Singer (Social
  Studies)
Paula Vaillant (French)

DICTION

Edith Braun (German)
Evelina Colorni (Italian)

Madeleine Marshall (English)
René Vaillant (French)

DANCE

Martha Hill (Director)
Margaret Craske
Agnes de Mille
Martha Graham
Louis Horst
Doris Humphrey
Ann Hutchinson
Helen Lanfer
José Limon
Antony Tudor
Robert P. Cohan (Assistant)

Alfredo Corvino (Assistant)
Ruth Currier (Assistant)
June Dunbar (Assistant)
Mattlyn Gavers (Assistant)
Els Grelinger (Assistant)
Betty Jones (Assistant)
Yuriko Kikuchi (Assistant)
Helen McGehee (Assistant)
Natanya Neumann (Assistant)
Lucy Venable (Assistant)
Ethel Winter (Assistant)

This listing does not include members of the Faculties of the School's Extension and Preparatory Divisions.

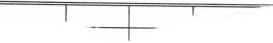

DATE DUE

A fine of TEN CENTS will be charged for
each day the book is kept overtime.